Raising Happy
and
Successful Kids

Raising Happy and Successful Kids

and

by *Adele M. Brodkin, Ph. D.*

A Guide for Parents

ISBN 0-439-07174-7

12 11 10 9 8 7 6 5 4 3 2 1   6 7 8 9 10 11/0

Printed in the U.S.A.
First printing, September 2006

For Billy, Rob, Lexi, and Charlie
—A.M.B.

INTRODUCTION

Over my many years as an adviser to Scholastic's Web site and *Parent and Child* magazine, I have answered hundreds of questions from concerned parents about the development of their children. This book is a collection of some of my favorite and most frequently asked questions, covering such topics as family life, child care, and education.

I have found that if we, as parents and grandparents, remember three core truths, we will be able to handle almost any situation that comes up with our young children.

The first is that from infancy on, every healthy person has a strong desire for autonomy. That is why we can expect to guide our children, but we cannot expect to completely control them. The sooner we appreciate that fact, the fewer power struggles we will have.

Secondly, children (and adults, too) have a strong need for attachment. While they seek independence, they need to know that they are loved and safe. So, for example, the same toddler who insists "Me do it" or whose favorite word seems to be no, shows just as strong a need for parental approval and hugs.

Finally, young children are happiest when they feel listened to and understood. We are wise to presume nothing, but instead, tune in, observe, and listen intently to what our children tell us, whether with gestures, language, or through play. There are times when we must be firm in limit-setting to keep them safe and at ease in their surroundings. But it helps to show even the youngest children that we understand how they feel.

The art of parenting involves tuning in to the needs and desires of each family member and trusting your judgment about how to balance them all justly. In this chapter, we consider questions about the parenting advice of others, about sibling rivalry, about empathy for adopted children, and more. We aim to guide parents toward discovering what may be best in any given moment for any given child.

When Others Tell You How to Parent

Q: My mother-in-law thinks we are making bad decisions in raising our child because our little girl is still on a bottle at thirteen months and we don't force her to take two naps a day. This same grandmother says we demand too much of our child if we bring her along when we go shopping or visiting. Our daughter seems happy, secure, smart, and outgoing, but my mother-in-law sets off feelings of doubt. Please give us your advice.

Q: My son just turned two and my friends say he should be potty-trained, and that it's my fault that he is not. I thought I had learned the hard way. I tried training my daughter on and off from the age of two without success. The day after her third birthday, she decided on her own that she didn't need diapers anymore. Should I listen to my friends, or decide what to do based on my own experience?

Q: I have several friends who home-school their children, and they are pressuring me to do the same with my five-year-old son. I have read to him every day since he was a year old and I teach him a lot, but I don't know whether I feel comfortable doing it formally four hours a day, 180 days a year. Does that make me a neglectful mother?

A: *No one knows your child's needs better than you.* What do all these parents have in common? They have friends or relatives providing unsolicited advice to change their parenting styles, although the children are doing just fine. Not only are the self-appointed advisers intrusive, they may also be undermining competent parents' well-earned confidence. And that is a pity. With rare exceptions, no one knows your child's needs better than you.

In the introduction to his respected parenting book, Dr. Spock urged each parent to "trust yourself." Many parents need to hear that exhortation again. So I say, give little heed to self-appointed experts on what is best for your children. Instead, trust yourself. By the way, how many of the successful people you know have parents who could have predicted their success by the age the children walked or used the potty? To reassure yourself about the timing of such developmental events, consult one of the many fine expert-authored parenting books (I have listed some in the back of this book), and you will see that there is a broad range of "normal" timing.

Disagreeing with Relatives

Q: My mother-in-law watches my twenty-month-old son while I am at work, and whenever I see how she deals with him, I get very upset. She won't let him do things for himself because she is concerned about him getting dirty. She gets nervous when he spills or drops food, so she only gives him food that won't be messy. I tell her to let him experiment. She then argues that he doesn't need to do things himself. And it's not just food. She even makes him play on the cement outdoors just so he stays clean. He ends up getting frustrated and fusses, then she yells at him to stop. I don't know what to do.

A: *Trust your instincts.*

You are absolutely correct that your boy's inclination to explore whatever his senses discover is healthy and deserves encouragement. However, it's not unusual for there to be a clash between toddlers' urges to experiment, mush, spill, throw, etc., and some people's inclinations to be clean and cautious. It's possible that your mother-in-law has always been concerned about cleanliness, but now she's less flexible than ever. In short, your child needs another child-care arrangement.

Start looking around for good child-care personnel or programs, and when you find one that you are certain is of high quality and matches your child's temperament, somehow graciously get out of your present arrangement. Of course, you will need your husband's agreement. The two of you can find a nice way to show gratitude toward his mother — a gift, a trip, a party; and a statement that you've decided together it isn't fair to ask more of her, particularly now that the little one needs to be with other kids.

Returning to Work

Q: My husband and I have been home with our six-week-old baby since he was born. Now I must return to work, and soon after, my husband will as well. When he does, he and I will have opposite shifts for five days of the week and the same two days off together to spend as a family. We are both very loving and attentive to our baby, but I am worried that despite our best efforts, this won't be enough. As his mother, shouldn't I be with my child twenty-four hours a day? How will my full-time work schedule affect his development? Is a child who has shared care worse off than a baby whose mother can be with him full-time?

A: *Your husband is not just a kind substitute; he is a devoted parent.*
The love and devotion behind your question is very moving. But the question itself is difficult to answer. No two infant-mother situations are identical, and not all infants have the same needs. Even identical twins are not born with precisely the same temperament, need for nurturing, capacity for making attachments, or degree of flexibility. And not all mothers have the same needs, either. (Yes, mothers' needs should be

respected, too.) Assuming they even have a choice, many devoted mothers are refreshed by an opportunity to spend some time in the company of adults, while others are more comfortable being with their babies all day every day. And no one has shown unequivocally what is universally "best" for all mother-infant pairs.

Experts do seem to agree about one thing: Infants who have two reliable, responsive, loving adults sharing their care can do just as well as those who are cared for exclusively by their moms. And your son's situation is even better. Your husband is not just a kind substitute; he is a devoted parent. I can't imagine that any dad who is happy to share equally in his child's care would not be a loving caregiver. So you can rest assured that your son has a fine opportunity for healthy growth and development.

By the way, work is only one form of "responsibility." When there are older children, and perhaps, other relatives to care for, an infant does not have his mother's exclusive, undivided attention. Your baby, on the other hand, always has at least one of the two people who love him most in the world by his side. As long as his two parents are enjoying him and not feeling overwhelmed by too many responsibilities, he should thrive. Just don't forget to save some time for your husband and you to continue enjoying each other's company, as well.

Should We Have Another Child?

Q: We adore and enjoy our three-year-old daughter, and she is doing fine as far as we can tell. However, members of my family are pressuring me to have another child, which neither my husband nor I is eager to do. We are both approaching age forty and are truly satisfied with our little family. Is it bad for our daughter to be an only child?

A: *Only you know what's right for you.*
While these days, forty isn't too old to have a child, only you and your husband can say what's right for you. So let your well-wishers know that this decision is entirely yours. Extended family members may have the best of intentions, but no one has the right to make this choice for you.

In answer to your question about only children, there is no evidence that it is bad to be an only child. In fact, while there are certain advantages to having siblings, studies have shown that only children are more likely to be high achievers and more comfortable amusing themselves. And since they get exclusive adult attention and are included in more adult conversations, they are also more likely to have larger vocabularies and more mature speech and language. Recent research also shows that only children are not more likely to suffer socially.

Of course, it is a good idea to give your daughter lots of opportunities to be with other children in both structured and less structured situations — preschool, neighborhood, and park play with appropriate supervision. As she gets older, having play dates and special activities in addition to interests that involve other children will give her practice working out the inevitable interpersonal conflicts everyone encounters.

The Family Bed

Q: I have a four-year-old who still sleeps in bed with my husband and me. We have tried and tried to get him out, but he cries for hours and eventually we give in. What should we do?

Q: I am desperate! We have a six-year-old daughter who does not want to sleep in her own bedroom. She falls asleep in our bed, and we carry her in to her bed when she is asleep. Then, in the middle of the night, she comes back into our bed. We don't always have the energy to take her back. We have tried a reward system to induce her to stay in her room and tried removing from her room anything that might look scary in the dark. None of this works. We could use your help!

Q: When my son was a baby, I read about the value of the family bed. Since he was not a good sleeper and I had to get up in the morning to go to work, we put him in our bed at night. We have been fine with this until now. Our son is nine years old and still sleeping with us. He thinks this is where he belongs and is still scared of the dark. He panics if we're not there to sleep by him. What can we do?

A: *Learning to sleep alone is part of the process of normal growth.*

Perhaps it might help if we first consider what these struggles are all about. It is very understandable that many young children have trouble giving up the physical closeness of the adults they need and love at night. And it is understandable, too, that devoted, exhausted parents often give in.

From infancy on, we all wrestle with a conflict between the need for safety from emotional and physical closeness and the need to feel competent as separate individuals. It is perhaps our greatest challenge to build a life that balances the two. As parents, we perpetually face the even greater challenge of guiding our children to do the same. We want to protect them but don't wish to clip their wings, and it isn't easy to know what a particular child is ready for at a particular moment.

But few would disagree that the children referred to above would be better off sleeping alone in their own beds. For that degree of independence to be achieved, it is best to begin building it much earlier in children's lives. It's important for babies, toddlers, and young children to make friends with the night, to acquire a sense of themselves as separate individuals, and to tolerate nighttime aloneness. All children should be comforted by the knowledge that their parents are nearby and certain that they will all be reunited in the morning. This is all part of the major developmental work of early childhood.

The family bed idea, though romanticized recently, actually originated in times and places where there was nowhere else to sleep but together. Now there is. The family bed usually does not work for children in our culture, which ultimately expects every individual to function on her own. Old habits die hard, so it is best not to start out having children sleep in parents' beds. Instead, it is wise to be very alert to children's daytime clues about their feelings, fears, etc. By letting them see that we love and understand them during the day, we will be helping them to trust us enough to separate at night, confident that we will still be there in the morning. Then, too, if we allow them the reasonable freedom to make certain decisions within the bounds of safety — what to wear, what to play, what to eat — it will be easier for them to grow up enjoying their separateness as much as togetherness. In short, learning to trust one's parents and one's self enough to sleep alone is part of the process of normal growth.

Of course, young children are entitled to a calm household, reassuring bedtime rituals — a special song, a stuffed animal or blanket in their arms, a calming story such as *Goodnight Moon*, and hugs from parents with cheerful reminders of the fun that awaits them with you "tomorrow." And yes, it is normal for children to stall sometimes, with requests for extra drinks of water, one more story, etc.

So far I have offered some clues about preventing the bind that some parents find themselves in years later. But what about those who are already stuck in a pattern that they know must be changed? If your child is verbal enough to understand, I suggest trying this approach. Tell her that she is big enough to go to sleep in her own wonderful room. Then, after you've sung some lullabies and read a story, all in her room, it's okay to sit in a chair while she drifts off to sleep. If she is unable to settle down with you or her dad there, tell her you know she can do this grown-up thing, kiss her good night, and leave. You may have to steal yourself to her crying for a long time, for several nights. You can also offer her a night-light, lots of favorite stuffed animals, and assurance about being together in the morning, before you take your leave. Be firm, and don't forget to give her extra playtime with you during the day. And be sure there are no other changes in her life right now.

But this approach won't work with every child. Sometimes children who have missed opportunities to develop a separate sense of self may need expert help from trained and certified child mental-health professionals in order to progress toward age-appropriate independence. Such a person will get to know your child and you, and be able to offer both insights and practical suggestions.

When an Older Child Is Jealous

Q: My two-year-old son is always taking toys away from my eight-month-old daughter, not to keep for himself, just because he doesn't want her to have them. What can I do to encourage him to be kinder?

A: *By having another child, you didn't betray your son.*

He doesn't want his baby sister to have any toys, and he certainly doesn't want his parents to have her. Your son probably is wondering why he is not enough to fill your parenting needs. This is a very expectable response. Spock has compared the feelings of an older child to those of a wife whose husband comes home one day and says, "I'd like you to meet my new second wife. It has been so wonderful being married to you that I've decided to bring another woman home. We will all be living together as a family now. So be nice to her."

Of course, you and I know that by having another child, you didn't betray your son. In fact, the painful reality of having to share you will help him make interpersonal compromises in time, as well as bring him companionship and many other good things as the years go on. He's just too young to know that now. The best you can do is casually point out what he can do that the baby can't: help you cook, help his father with house repairs, ride a tricycle, eat pizza, push a little wagon in the market, etc.

Children of all ages may feel jealous of newborn siblings. One nine-and-a-half-year-old, who was no longer able to do fun mother-daughter things after school, like shop and eat at restaurants, insisted that the parent now loved the baby more. Another parent was concerned that her eight-year-old daughter would suffer throughout life from the trauma of having a needy new infant sibling. Parents in situations like these seem to feel guilty about what they have done to their older children. That is too bad and certainly not warranted.

Try making time alone for the older child. If there are two adults in the house, one can relieve the baby's primary caregiver while that parent does something special with the older child. Life isn't going to be the same for him. But, in the long run, that will not matter as much as having fun with his friends, being proud of his growing competence, and being the big brother.

When Siblings Fight

Q: I have two daughters, ages eight and five, who share a bedroom. When it's time to clean up, they both fight terribly. I have tried to give each of them a specific chore so they won't get overwhelmed. But they seem to enjoy setting each other off. Any suggestions?

A: *Stay out of it.*
   Yes. I am tempted to say that my suggestion has only four words: Stay out of it. But you are entitled to more than that, and I know how frustrating this is for parents. I've been there. So, first ask yourself a couple of questions: Do the girls have fun together at other times, and even occasionally look out for each other away from home? Is cleanup the primary time they battle? If your answer to these questions is yes, there is nothing for you to do but stay out of it. As long as

no one gets hurt and you make it perfectly clear that you will never tolerate physical attacks, as long as it stays verbal, it is their problem to resolve.

Incidentally, you might as well give up now on trying to get their room cleaned, or you'll be locked in an eternal struggle by early adolescence. Close the door on the mess and the fights, and let them work out who does what chore. If you refuse to be drawn in as referee or judge, the fighting will be very likely to lose its appeal.

Some sibling squabbling is absolutely normal and should be tolerated, on the condition that it is away from where you are. If, on the other hand, the fighting is constant, with no happy sisterly times, consider carefully why your children feel battling is acceptable (as is the case when parents themselves bicker and fight a lot) or the way to win acceptance and parental favor.

When an Older Child Is Bossy

Q: My five-year-old daughter is always playing Mom to her one-year-old sister. I think it's great that she is so protective, but I find myself constantly telling her that it is okay if the little one plays with this or that. I have tried to explain the value of allowing a toddler to explore, reassuring my older daughter that I am watching out for her safety. But even so, my five-year-old continues to be bossy. I know this is probably normal, but how can I get across to my eldest that she needs to let up?

A: *Diverting works better than confrontation.*

The bossiness of your older child is quite normal, and, yes, your toddler should have the freedom to explore under your watchful eyes. Perhaps it may help to consider the fact that your big girl is in a bind. She doesn't know where to go with her normal jealousy of and probable aggressive feelings toward her adorable and adored baby sister. She can't control the fact that this rival exists, so she tries to control the toddler herself.

Here are a few things you might try: Find about an hour a day to spend just with your older child, maybe during your toddler's nap or when Daddy or another relative can watch the younger. In that hour, give your full attention to your big girl. Join her and allow her to take the lead in dramatic play. She may express some of her frustration through the drama, which will give you a chance to acknowledge her feelings. Perhaps the two of you can also go off to a nearby park, an ice-cream store, or another fun spot, with her talking and you actively listening and reacting warmly. When you are back together with the younger, find tasks for your older child to do, ways for her to help you, or ways to continue with a game or activity that the little one can't do — painting at an easel or baking cookies, for example. Also, consider arranging play dates for your older child with other five-year-olds.

Raising children is without a doubt a continual challenge, but it might help to keep in mind that, in this case and many others, diverting works better than confrontation.

Respecting Each Child's Uniqueness

Q: My husband and I are aware of the importance of reading to children, beginning in infancy. We read to our first child early. She is now five and loves books. Our fifteen-month-old son is a different story! We've tried reading to him, but either he won't sit still, grabs the book, or tries to turn back to the beginning. Sometimes he'll even get up and walk away. Do you have any suggestions? We really want him to grow up enjoying books as much as his sister does.

A: *Respect your child's individuality.*

I am so glad that you asked this question because it gives us an opportunity to talk about much more than the importance of reading. In answer to your request for suggestions, I would say that it is vital to follow your toddler's lead. At fifteen months, if he is more of an action guy than a sit-and-read-one-page-at-a-time guy, that is just fine, and it is not wise to fight it. It doesn't necessarily mean that he won't end up sharing a number of his sister's and parents' interests, but he will and should follow his own inclinations in the pursuit of joy. Autonomy and action, the delight of free movement, may be what appeals to him now and possibly for a good long time.

You can give him all the opportunities that you are giving to his sister, but the most important of those opportunities is to be accepted and admired for himself. If books are around, he is likely to come to them at his own pace. If he sees the rest of you reading, he will know that reading is highly valued. As his interests develop more, I'd suggest that you find books relating to those interests and keep them nearby. They may not all be classics, although if he becomes interested in heavy machinery or trains, as many preschool-age boys do, *Mike Mulligan and His Steam Shovel* and *The Little Engine That Could* are great additions to any young child's library. But don't push those, either. Pressing the point could even have the opposite effect.

The essence of my suggestion is that the most precious gift any parent can give to any child is respect for that child's individuality. We need all kinds of talents and interests to make our world go around. So have a great time getting to know each of your children as separate and equally valued individuals. Guide and encourage them as appropriate, but let them know you are fascinated by and proud of the person each is now, and is becoming.

Demanding More of One Child Than Another

Q: I have two children, a boy who is seven and a girl who is five. I love them both, but sometimes I feel that I am more demanding of the older one. I'm just not sure if I'm being fair. What advice can you give me?

A: *We don't get to choose our birth order or our parents.*
   Over years of working with children and families, I have observed that parents are often less relaxed

and possibly most demanding of their first children. It almost seems as if the first child represents the parent herself or himself, while the younger ones are "just kids." If there is any validity to this observation, it may mean that we do expect more of our first children. However, there are some positive consequences. First children tend to be high achievers and more demanding of themselves, therefore inclined to get things done. But does this mean that the older child is cheated of leniency, that the younger one is cheated of high standards, or neither?

I vote neither. As long as a parent is tuned into each child, loving, consistent, and, of course, never abusive, fairness is not an issue. Life is a roulette wheel. We don't get to choose our birth order or our parents. Most children are quite resilient and make the most of their lot. What's more, the fact that you are questioning all of this suggests to me that you are a reflective person (maybe a first child yourself), and clearly a concerned, caring parent. Keep an eye on all of this, and if your doubts continue, you might want to seek counseling with an expert on parent-child relationships. In the meantime, enjoy your family.

My Adopted Child Doesn't Look Like Me

Q: My husband and I adopted our son from Vietnam when he was three months old. We've always been honest with him about his adoption and talked freely about his having two countries. But recently, at his preschool, another child asked him why he didn't look like me, and I have noticed a change in his behavior. He refuses to go outside to play after school, and he's made some comments about not having a "real mom." We couldn't love any child more than we do our son. How can we help him?

A: *You are his real and forever family.*

No child wants to be different from those around him, yet part of growing up is discovering and becoming comfortable with one's uniqueness. Adopted children may find this particularly challenging, especially if there are different racial or ethnic origins within the family. But sensitive and loving parents, like you and your husband, have a head start on guiding your child over the hurdles.

I don't mean to dismiss the challenges a family faces, challenges that will wax and wane at different phases of your boy's development. You have seen already that questions about your son's adoption are bound to come up in and out of school. As he grows older, more questions will arise in his own mind about who he is and where he belongs. That is developmentally inevitable, so try to take it in stride.

There are some concrete things you can do. Inviting friends of Asian origin and children who were also adopted from Vietnam to your home will allow your son to be with adults and children whose backgrounds are similar to his own. And collecting art or photographs of Vietnam, along with reading children's books about the country and books about adoption, will allow him to grow up around images that reflect him, his birth land, and his adoption. But through it all, the most important thing you can both do directly and indirectly is to reassure him that you are his real and forever family.

Should Parents Play Differently with Boys and Girls?

Q: My husband is hesitant to roughhouse with our four-year-old daughter the way he does with our sons. He seems to think that little girls should just play quietly with dolls. I grew up in a household of all girls. We had fun roughhousing and playing with boys' toys as well as girls'. So to me, it seems a shame that our daughter is missing out. How can I help my husband understand it's best to treat sons and daughters the same way?

A: *Take your lead from whatever appeals to her.*
    Each boy or girl is unique. So first, let's consider the perspective of the central person — your daughter. Some girls do prefer quiet doll play to tree climbing or roughhousing. Others are just the opposite or somewhere in between. (And, of course, some boys are more inclined to play board games, build with Lincoln logs, or draw than wrestle.) Just because a girl prefers dress-up play to football doesn't mean she is any less likely to become a surgeon, engineer, or explorer when she grows up. What is most likely to influence her future willingness to take positive risks and climb life's highest mountains is a quiet sense of having been accepted, valued, and enjoyed just as she is. So I

advise getting to know your daughter and joining her in whatever kind of play she chooses to do. Of course, as time goes on, offering her all sorts of opportunities for learning and developing skills in sports, as well as more sedentary activities is fine — as long as you and her dad take your lead from whatever appeals to her. If she doesn't love field hockey, but she does love horseback riding or drama, be proud and encouraging. Ideally, parents offer opportunities, then watch with great interest how their children choose to express their individuality.

But there is another part of your question that I would like to address, and that is, your suggestion that fathers should treat their daughters exactly as they treat their sons. While I agree that girls and boys deserve equal love, admiration, and respect, there is often an intuitive difference between the way we relate to children of the opposite sex and children of our own sex, and that is really okay. In fact, it can be helpful for fathers to treat their daughters with a certain gentleness and sweetness, preparing their girls to expect nothing less from the men who may someday be important in their lives.

Parenting is never dull and frequently it's full of surprises. As one parent lamented, "Just when I think I have them figured out, they change!" In this chapter, we confront parents' questions about their children's often puzzling behavior. As children grow and the demands on them grow, too, how should parents answer their children's unsettling questions? What is the best way to address their fears while helping them remain in charge of their own lives?

Life with a Toddler

Q: I have a lot of questions about my two-year-old's behavior. First of all, he is not interested in potty-training and, lately, he is such a picky eater. I have tried all kinds of foods, but he will eat only some. And then after a few bites, he loses interest. He doesn't speak in full sentences yet, only words and a lot of gesturing to get what he wants. When he doesn't get his way, he sometimes has a tantrum. I am not sure what to do about any of these things. Can you help?

A: *Hang in there.*
Congratulations! You are the mother of a typical two-year-old. Nothing you have described worries me at all. In fact, it is quite nice to hear about such a normal little guy. I know you're thinking: *That's easy for you to say....* But I truly am sympathetic. It is a tough age because normally developing children are struggling with a typical two-year-old conflict between a

strong urge to be independent and a need for parental protection. What is more, many two-year-olds feel frustrated about not being able to communicate the urgency of their wishes. As you said, your boy's use of formal language is just developing, and he's in a hurry to be understood. It is wonderful that he uses gestures and even single words to get what he wants. Keep those lines of communication going, whether he uses words, sentences, or gestures. It's communication itself that matters for his future emotional, social, and cognitive development.

As for the potty, put it aside and bring it out in a couple of months. There is no use in having a power struggle over that, especially because you can't win.

His eating habits are not worrisome, either. Again, avoid power struggling to prevent problems. Give him what he likes, even if it's peanut butter and tomatoes three times a day. Every now and then, introduce a taste of something new. Expect him to reject it. Limit snacks unless you feel they are nutritious. If he comes to the table hungry, he's likely to get what he needs. Don't coax. Just allow a half-hour maximum for eating, then clean up and move on to something else. Consult your pediatrician or family doctor at the next checkup about all of this, and about how much milk and/or juice he is having, and whether it is too much of either or not enough.

When it comes to tantrums, do your best not to join in. Stay calm, state your limits, be sure he is in a safe place to kick and scream, and tell him you will be there when he is finished. I am not suggesting that you walk out on him, but that you give yourself a respite, by turning to other things — cooking, reading, paperwork, as long as you can keep one eye on his safety.

Last, but not least, hang in there; all these things will change in time. And when he's a grown-up, he'll never believe it all happened. You and I will know the truth.

Worrying About Monsters

Q: My thirty-month-old son has recently begun to worry about monsters. It began one night, when just before going to bed, he said there was a monster in a fort in his bedroom. When I tried to explain that monsters are just pretend, he didn't seem to understand. So I turned on the light and showed him there was no monster, then kissed him good night. A few minutes later, he called out that there was. I asked if he wanted me to take the fort out of the room, and he did. A few days later, he said there are monsters everywhere: in his room, outside, in the living room, in the basement. He starts out by saying they are nice monsters and then later says he's scared of them. What should I do to help my son through this? And what should I not be doing?

A: *With your reassurance, this phase is likely to pass soon.*
What you should not do is worry. Your son is quite precocious. Most children don't have the imagination

to think up monsters until at least about a year later. And even fewer have his verbal ability to describe the fears or to try to reassure themselves by calling the monsters "nice." The concept of real versus pretend is still beyond him, though. In fact, at his age, even his dreams seem to have been real events. So he is both blessed and stuck with this rich imagination, without an older child's at least partial understanding that it's make-believe. But as long as his actual life is calm, as long as he knows his important adults are reliably there for him, reliably loving and tuned in to him, there aren't many things to caution you about.

I would advise lots of free playtime with you as his play partner, letting him be the director. Welcome his bossing you around in the play, as long as it is safe play. He may act out conflicts between soldiers in the fort who represent his own wishes for power and his own fears of being aggressive or a sense of being small and vulnerable. With your reassurance, allowing him to be in charge during pretend play and read-ing lots of stories with warm feelings, as well as your evident pleasure in him, this phase is likely to pass soon. At bedtime, he may need a night-light and lots of reassurance about how much you love him and are there to protect him. Also, you can remind him about the fun you'll have together tomorrow.

"Mommy, Where Do Babies Come From?"

Q: My four-year-old twins were recently introduced to a new baby cousin. That started a flurry of questions about where babies come from. I answered, "Babies grow in a very special place in their mommies' tummies." Then, a few days later, my son asked if the mommy's belly button was opened to get the baby out. And my daughter asked how she and her twin brother got into my belly. I wasn't sure what to say, so I changed the subject. What information about sex can children handle at their age?

Q: My eight-year-old daughter has asked questions in the past about where babies come from. I have explained about pregnancy in detail, but now she wants to know how the baby gets there to begin with. What is the right age for children to have sex education?

A: *Answer what is asked, no more and no less.*

I think it's a good idea to heed the advice of a distinguished child therapist, the late Selma Fraiberg, who recommended asking the questioning child for his own theories before plunging into an answer. In the first question, the boy twin has already stated his assumption that the mommy's belly button had to be opened to let the baby out. This misimpression should be gently corrected. "No, that's not what happens. What other ideas do you have about how the baby gets out?" Each incorrect assumption can be respectfully corrected, and then the actual facts should be presented using proper terminology.

When the girl twin is asked what she thinks about how the baby got inside the mommy, she is likely to express another common theory of young children — the mommy swallowed or ate something that made it happen. Parents who offer the explanation of the daddy planting the seed often hear it played back with their children's fantasy of the mommy taking the seed, like a pill, with a glass of water.

With the eight-year-old girl, your role is not only to provide accurate facts but also reassurance about her future as a woman. But no matter how meticulous your explanations may be, children are still likely to draw their own creative conclusions. Nevertheless, we would do best not to act amused. Instead, explain the facts, answering exactly what is asked as clearly and calmly as possible. Many children come back again and again for further clarification. That will give you additional chances to correct earlier distortions and misimpressions.

In sum, listen carefully to children's questions about sex. Once you know what they are really asking, answer what is asked, no more and no less. Respond with complete candor, in language that your child can understand. By leaving the door open for a continuing, relaxed, and loving dialogue, you will be helping your child feel pleased about his own gender identity. Don't worry about telling too much; children have a way of "not hearing" what they are not ready to hear. Children need to know that you are comfortable with their very normal curiosities, and that there is no topic that they cannot feel comfortable asking you about.

Fear of Animals

Q: I have a four-year-old girl who is afraid of both dogs and cats. We can't go outside in the neighborhood without some animal causing her to be very frightened. Because I respect her fear, she and I are the laughingstock of our family and friends. What should I do?

Q: My seven-year-old son is afraid of dogs. He will not go to his best friend's house if their dog is not tied up. He will not go to my brother's house at all because they have a dog. We even have to cross the street if a dog is on the same side we are walking on. We have been very sensitive, trying not to push. Instead, we talk about what a dog does when it first meets you — sniffing, licking, maybe jumping. Our son has made a little progress — he's even willing to touch our neighbor's puppy — but I am concerned about him and worried that his fear is rubbing off on our four-year-old twins. What can we do?

A: *Fear of animals is quite common.*

If either child has ever been bitten, scratched, attacked, or knocked over by a dog (or cat, in the girl's case), it may take longer to get over the fear, but it can ease up in time. The parents need to keep listening to whatever their child has to say about being scared. With the younger child, that might be easier to do through play. (Using stuffed animals, the child may show what is scary about the feared animal.) Imaginary play in your calm, accepting presence is a good antidote. But don't expect an instantaneous "cure." Then, too, if you, yourself, are not frightened by the animals, your child's fear is more likely to diminish.

Fear of animals is quite common, particularly among preschool children who don't have a pet. Since both of the parents who sent these questions are tuned in to their children, they are likely to know if the timing happens to be right for acquiring a family pet. Not only is it essential to sense that the child is ready (by seeing the boy's positive reaction to the neighbor's puppy, for example), but a lot of research and family soul searching needs to be done before going ahead. Be sure that a pet will not be a burden for a busy family and that the breed you select is calm and accepting of children, as well as highly trainable. Then decide who is going to do the training. For the little girl, when she is ready, a small kitten might be the better choice. In any case, having a pet that becomes a loved family member may help a child to master a once overwhelming fear. Just be sure the timing is right for all concerned.

Suddenly Afraid of Going to Sleep

Q: My five-year-old daughter has recently started throwing fits at bedtime. When I tell her it is time to brush teeth and get her "jammies" on, she says she has a scary feeling and points to her belly. My husband and I have tried everything we can think of, but we can't seem to ease her fears. We have stayed and read stories, sung songs, prayed together, and we have also tried the quick good-night approach. Nothing works. She still screams and demands that I be with her until she falls asleep. Then everything is fine for the rest of the night. We are puzzled since this never happened when she was younger.

A: *Bedtime fears are common, too.*
Sudden emergence of bedtime fears is quite common. Stressful events — the birth of a baby, a divorce, a move, a change in caregivers or school, a family illness, a strain in the parents' marriage — can be precipitants of children's sleep difficulties, just as they can for adults. So, too, can a child's own inner conflict, jealousy, fear of reprisal from angry feelings, etc. Returning family life to its former calmness and predictability, if possible, and tuning in to the child's feelings expressed in daytime play are likely to help. If not, don't hesitate to consult an expert.

Some children fall into nighttime troubles after an illness, which brought Mommy or Daddy into their rooms for needed care. If that is the case, once the child is well, explain that now she is able to sleep throughout the night. Experts disagree about the merits of night-lights and open bedroom doors. Use your own judgment about what would work in your family. And when you respond to a child's middle-of-the-night call, keep your visit short and avoid turning on lights and doing activities together like reading or playing that belong to the daytime. Once you are assured that your child is well, let her know that now is the time for restful sleep to get ready for tomorrow, which promises to be another wonderful day.

The Big-kid Bed

Q: My three-year-old son is having a rough transition into his big-boy bed. I don't want to make it a big issue, but I also want him to get the sleep he needs. What do you suggest?

A: *Moving into a big-boy bed can be a shared effort.*
Young children do best if they feel they have some part in the decision to take meaningful steps toward growing up. Such steps are always a mixed bag, exciting in the freedom they offer, but with the cost of giving up some familiar pleasure or comfort. We see this when children are weaned from breast or bottle to the cup and again when diapers are given up and replaced with the potty and big-boy or -girl underwear. Introduction to the big-boy (or -girl) bed presents a similar dilemma. Parents who offer opportunities to take such steps toward growth gradually, and don't abruptly make the decisions for their child, often find the transition goes relatively well.

I suggest leaving both the crib and the big-boy bed in your boy's room for a few weeks, allowing him to experiment with the bed, before committing himself to it. Just as ideal weaning is gradual and a collaborative effort of parent and child, moving into a big-boy bed can be a shared effort, ultimately allowing the child to make the leap and discover the pleasures of personal mastery.

Self-soothing Habits

Q: My four-year-old son has begun to bite his nails. How can I nip this bad habit in the bud?

Q: My granddaughter is almost six and still sucks her thumb at night while she holds her special blanket. How can I help end her "baby" behavior?

A: *These habits are tension reducers and typically wane over time.*

For some reason, adults feel that it is our responsibility to put a stop to what we tend to term *annoying habits*. However, these behaviors which can also include sniffing, fidgeting, hair twisting or twirling, crossing and uncrossing fingers, and leg swinging are all extremely common among young children. They are tension reducers. Young children are often tense from the normal stresses of growing up. In and of themselves, the habits do not suggest serious trouble and typically wane when children find other ways of reducing stress.

It is important to ask yourself whether your child's habit is interfering with his living a full life. Does he enjoy friends, school, outside activities, or does pursuit of the habit take precedence? How long has the habit been there? Is it a response to a change in the child's environment? Are there increasing demands for compliant behavior in school or day care?

If your child has a rich, full life, unaffected by the occasional stress-reducing habit, simply ignore it, expecting it to wane over time. If, on the other hand, there are things going on at home or at school that create avoidable stress, of course, it is best to intervene on your child's behalf. If the habit is longstanding, it may take some time to wane, but behavior that is short-lived will often dissipate, once the stressor disappears. And you may never know what the stressor was. It could have simply been some brief developmental growing pains.

And since the habits mentioned here often represent a way of coping with angry feelings about having to comply, I advise ignoring them rather than trying to impose your own will on your child's choices about such matters. Instead, seize every opportunity to offer choices about simple everyday issues — whether to wear the blue or the green shirt, sneakers or sandals, have pancakes or waffles, etc. Let children pick the games you will play together, design the free play you'll do with them, the book you will read aloud, and the video or CD-ROM game you'll enjoy together. Save your firm stands for matters of safety and well-being. That's a good way to reduce tension between you and your growing child.

Difficulty with Losing

Q: If she loses at a game, my almost-four-year-old daughter won't play anymore. What can I do to teach her that losing is part of playing games, and that it is something we all experience in a competitive society?

A: *Be patient.*

Young children are not only innately egocentric; they aren't able to think ahead. There is no "Wait until next year!" in their cognitive repertoire. In fact, "Now! Right now!" is more typical of their thinking. Living in the competitive society you point to makes winning feel even more vital. It is in children's media and all around them in everyday life.

What is more, your daughter's refusal to lose is typical of many children her age. Threes, and even fours, are notorious for stomping off when they are not declared winners. There are lots of reasons: First of all, we humans are not born knowing how to share or how to accept even temporary defeat philosophically. These are learned qualities, socially invented to sustain social order. Children acquire them only gradually by witnessing others, as well as experiencing the rewards of appreciation bestowed for such behavior.

So be patient, model the qualities you hope to see in your child, reward her with loads of praise when she does accept even the slightest temporary defeat or compromise, and praise others who do the same. Praise her determination as well. Parents ask too much of themselves when they expect their young children to share adult logic and values before they have been seasoned by time, experience, and brain maturation.

Friendship Problems

Q: My second grader came home from school saying that she has no friends and no one likes her. This doesn't happen all the time, but when it does, it really breaks my heart.

A: *The trouble may soon become a thing of the past.*
I am glad to hear that your daughter's sense of being friendless is only a sometimes thing. At her age, children who have had a rough day often forget yesterday's good times. So if she wasn't chosen to be a partner of her presumed "best friend" today, or if two of her friends decided to go off and whisper on the playground and leave her out, she is likely to have forgotten that she was an insider yesterday and very likely will be again tomorrow. In her case, the sense of being a social failure may therefore be unwarranted.

Nevertheless, I would suggest that you meet with her teacher, to get an observant adult's viewpoint about what is really going on. If it turns out that your daughter is having some social difficulties, together, you and the teacher might figure out what the stumbling block is. And if you can establish an ongoing collaborative relationship, share observations, and plan ways of addressing any obvious reasons for your child's shaky social acceptance, the trouble may soon become a thing of the past. You can also invite friends over for play dates after school, and keep your eyes and ears open for possible origins of any problem.

If, however, a child *is* consistently socially isolated, professional intervention is needed. Being truly friendless is at least as worrisome as having persistent academic or learning problems. As a matter of fact, there is a positive association between persistent social isolation in the primary years and future school failure. So that level of difficulty would warrant a consultation with a board-certified child psychiatrist or child psychologist.

Copying Negative Role Models

Q: My four-year-old son goes to preschool three days a week. He and I both love the program. But I am concerned that my son is attracted to and easily influenced by a few other children who, the teachers and I agree, are not positive role models. There is one boy in particular who is nine months older and very uncooperative, refusing to participate in many of the activities. While my son still clearly has a positive attitude toward group activities, he imitates the older boy's habits of name calling and hitting himself over the head. I am concerned about my child's apparent suggestibility as well as his inability to know which behaviors are okay to imitate. I've been talking to him about what not to copy and encouraging him to play with many of the other children in the class, but there has been no dramatic change. Do you have any suggestions?

A: *You are still the strongest influence in your son's life.*

Many parents of young children share your concerns, and although they recognize that copying another young child's negative behaviors may be rather harmless, they wonder if doing so forecasts suggestibility to bad influences in later childhood and adolescence. It is an understandable concern, but one that is probably not warranted. First of all, there are big differences in the moral aptitudes of four- and fourteen-year-olds. Preschoolers still have rather primitive consciences, a limited sense of right and wrong. For the most part, they behave the way we ask them to in order to please us or avoid displeasing us, rather than because of their own standards and values. Often, some like your son, who are model citizens, leap at the opportunity to do some unacceptable things, when another child seems to have cleared the path.

I think you are very wise to devalue the older child's behavior and to encourage other friendships. Don't worry about whether you are getting your message across. You are. You are still the strongest influence in your son's life, and if the data we have is to be trusted, you still will be when he is an adolescent. That is not always obvious because children are eager to find models and heroes of their own gender and closer to their age, but you can gently guide your child toward heroes that you, too, can admire. That combined with your loving encouragement for his growing skills, talents, and jobs well done as well as attunement to his feelings will continue to assure your place as the number-one role model in his life.

Is My Daughter Becoming a Liar?

Q: We have a wonderful five-year-old daughter whose imagination is running wild. I'm afraid that what might once have been storytelling has become lying. For example, she said that two neighborhood children don't like her or want to play with her. According to the other girls, they never said that. So I punished my daughter by putting her in a time-out and forbade her to play with the other children for the rest of the afternoon. She said she learned her lesson, but later she lied again about the matter. This time, I punished her by prohibiting outdoor play for one whole day. What is happening to our sweet little girl? Why is she lying?

A: *Punishment is by far the least effective method of changing behavior.*

Children of this age have a different notion of reality from adults. They often *undo* things in their own minds or blow them up out of proportion, which is not the same as willful lying by an older child or adult. In order to understand and guide your daughter, it is important to be aware of this developmental distinction. I am not sure that we know what really happened or who is bending the truth, if anyone. How do you know, for example, whether the other two girls are denying what might indeed have happened, especially since it is such a common scenario with young children? Three is often a crowd. One of the two other little girls might have said something like, "If you . . . then I won't be your friend" or "won't play with you ever again!" The moment could have passed, so to them, it didn't happen. If that were the case, they, too, would not be lying.

But perhaps none of these things ever happened. Instead, your daughter might have just felt unwanted and unliked by them, without objective cause; she might not have wanted to play with them, or maybe, she only wanted to play with one of the children. Then, too, she might even have preferred to be with you. In any of these cases, she wouldn't have been lying, but rather dealing with her world and her needs in the only way she feels she can.

One more heartfelt suggestion: If we want to enable our children to be socially competent, taking away opportunities to play with other children is not the wisest course. In fact, the more chances your daughter can have to work out and prevent little squabbles the better, which means the chance for more peer play, not less. I must admit, too, that I usually take a dim view of time-outs. It's fine to have a few minutes to "cool off" or "get some space" after a conflict, but isolation does not allow a useful lesson in communicating and relating. One last point — punishment is by far the least effective method of changing behavior. Reward for a job well done works so much better. I know, parenting isn't easy. In fact, the best-kept cultural secret is that it takes a lot more careful thinking than most of life's pursuits.

Role-playing

Q: Both my four-year-old and my six-year-old are fascinated with role-playing. They like to dress up in pretend costumes. Is this typical of kids their ages? Why would they crave trying on other identities?

A: *The benefits of pretend play are endless.*

Not only is your children's behavior not worrisome, it is cause for celebration, a sign of their healthy development, and a reason to be optimistic about their continuing social, emotional, and intellectual growth. I am grateful to you for asking the question, for it gives us an opportunity to share the good news about pretend play with other parents. Despite hundreds of articles, books, conferences, and expert pronouncements about the merits of play, especially imaginative play, many people continue to view it as frivolous, seeking to substitute rote academic exercises. That is an unfortunate cultural error, probably compounded now by our current focus on educational standards. The fact is, to meet meaningful "standards," what young children truly need is an opportunity for richer and richer pretend play, for it's an avenue to discovering what it feels like to be someone other than one's self. A well-developed capacity to put one's self in another person's place is a predictor of success, in love and in work. By pretending to be a mommy, daddy, teacher, police officer, doctor, or even power character, children are seeing the world from many perspectives, safely experiencing a broad range of emotions, coming to terms with fears and any sense of powerlessness or sadness while enjoying being in complete control of their pretend world. Problem-solving skills are enhanced as is creativity, a willingness to take appropriate risks by trying new things and developing new skills, including the give-and-take of social interaction and even motor skills. The storytelling component of imaginary play is an important preliteracy experience. So the benefits of pretend play are endless. Parents and teachers can provide some props, which don't have to be expensive costumes or toys; in fact, discarded clothing and other household items are often better. But adults should never take over control of the play. A pointed question here or there can help to extend the play into broader spheres of imagination, but as long as they are safe, the children should be in full charge.

So, in answer to your question, my advice is to sit back, relax, and enjoy the splendid show that is a tribute to your children's healthy growth.

Anger and Younger Children

Q: Our nineteen-month-old daughter has been acting aggressive both at home and at day care, where she has been hitting other children. She also pulled another child's hair and pushed someone. What do we do?

Q: My husband and I have different parenting styles, and that's a problem when it comes to disciplining our two-year-old son. I tend to be more strict and consistent; my husband tends to comfort and distract our boy. When he throws food, hits, or has a crying tantrum, my husband seems to make light of these aggressive or angry outbursts. I think he's let our child manipulate him, and I'm concerned that he doesn't understand that what we do will affect our son for the rest of his life.

Q: My nephew of seventeen months pulls hair, slaps, and is mean to other children, and seems to derive pleasure from it. Our whole family agrees that this behavior is detestable, but we don't know how to curb it.

Q: I have an almost two-year-old daughter who often gets angry and can be terribly destructive. She seems to enjoy breaking things so I have to watch her every minute. I feel embarrassed to visit friends' homes because of her behavior. This is new to me since my six-year-old son, at her age, was (and still is) quite docile. I don't know what to do.

A: *Encourage the safe expression of anger.*
Anger is a normal human emotion, and none of us was born knowing how to or when to hide angry or aggressive feelings. Then, too, some children do have more aggressive drive than others. It takes time, developmental growth, and patient guidance to redirect that drive into its potential for highly productive activity. What's more, at certain points in our children's development, we can expect to see more angry outbursts and uninhibited aggression than at others.

Between the ages of one and three, children frequently enjoy what we adults call destructiveness, and they do not disguise their occasional pleasure in hurting others. But by the time a child is five or six, we can expect most of her anger or hurtful feelings to be expressed verbally. If the anger goes completely underground, though, it can eventually create inner turmoil; so we try to encourage the safe expression of even negative feelings and show even preverbal children that we understand what they are feeling.

All other things being equal (and they never are, of course), the younger the child, the less worrisome aggressive behavior is. We expect a child of nineteen months to defend her newfound autonomy, and since she is not likely to have great command of oral language, she chooses the language of action. That doesn't mean we just let her go on hitting, pushing, or pulling hair. The adult in charge must firmly declare no to such behavior, while realizing that such admonitions alone will not make the desired change. Let it be clear to the child that you disapprove and won't allow her to hurt others, but know that the passage of time, which allows normal growth and development of language and frustration tolerance, is on your side. Recognize that self-interest, rather than politeness, comes naturally, and only gradually — after patient and consistent limit setting — will young children redirect their aggression safely and appropriately.

I know this is all very tough on parents. How can you know what is expectable, acceptable, or normal? What should you do if your child's behavior still seems intolerable? It might help to consult one of the many fine child-development handbooks. (I've listed a few at the end of this book.) At least, you may be reassured to see that your child's behavior is not unusual for her age and has clear developmental roots. She is not headed for a life of crime, based on what you are witnessing.

Of course, parents and teachers must set limits, prohibiting behavior that can be physically hurtful or destructive. Sometimes that can only be accomplished by removing the young child from the scene of the trouble. Try to anticipate and prevent problems by "staying out of china shops" with toddlers. Calmly and consistently let your feelings about aggressive behavior be known. It will sink in eventually. In the meantime, make an effort to tune in to underlying frustrations (such as jealousy of a sibling or the wish to accomplish some physical feat that is still beyond the little one's skills) that bring on the outbursts. Sympathize with your child's feelings, while prohibiting unacceptable acting out. Offer lots of harmless opportunities for your child to be in charge—for example, during play or with simple chores. And don't be impatient with yourself for feeling angry, as long as you, too, find acceptable ways of expressing it. The example you set may turn out to be the most important influence of all.

Aggressive Behavior in Three- to Eight-year-olds

Q: I have a three-year-old girl who is usually outgoing and happy. But when she is angry with me, she will lash out and hit. The outbursts usually occur when she has been overloaded with activities or she's tired (for example, when it is time to go home after playing in the park or at someone's house). I have done everything I can to stop this behavior, but nothing works. Sometimes, she pushes my buttons so much that I get angry and yell. Then I feel sorry and worry that I am harming her. What advice do you have?

Q: My five-year-old has a horrible temper. He blows up at the slightest thing that goes wrong. For example, when he is asked to stop doing something, he will often stomp off and say, "Fine. That's it. . . ." My husband finds this behavior especially unacceptable and wants to punish him for the outbursts. But I feel if we ride it out and show no emotion, our son will stop. We also have a two-year-old daughter who is sometimes the butt of our boy's anger.

Q: My son is seven and is constantly in trouble at school. He has always played rough with his older cousins (or they with him). Now the principal at his school says he is picking on other kids, but when I ask him about it, he says he was just playing. We have discussed proper school behavior, but he still gets in trouble. How should I handle this?

A: *Consider what frustrations are behind aggressive behavior.*
    Similar seeming aggressive behavior may have many different possible origins. In all situations, though, we need to remember that self-interest, rather than politeness and consideration, comes naturally, and only gradually, after patient and consistent limit

setting and positive role modeling by adults, will young children redirect their aggression safely and appropriately.

To the parents of the three-year-old who loses control when she is fatigued or abruptly separated from fun play: Along with your firm guidance, alert your daughter to the fact that the time is coming when play must end for today. Some children need several warnings, so start a half an hour ahead. Incidentally, occasional raising of your voice is not necessarily bad, if that is the way to get your unequivocal message across to a toddler or three-year-old. If you yell frequently, or are out of control yourself, though, your actions will lose their effect.

By age six or seven, most children have found ways to channel aggression and have learned to inhibit destructive impulses. But as the parent of the seven-year-old points out: Personal experience means a lot. It is possible that this boy really does think that very rough behavior characterizes all kids' play, since this is what he has experienced with his cousins. Then, too, he has been the low man on that front, so now he may be picking on others the way he has felt picked on. Child counseling or social skill lessons may be necessary to enable him to unlearn the inappropriate behavior. Certainly, less time should be spent with the rough cousins and more with peers who are willing to get together for cooperative play.

It may help to consider what frustrations are behind aggressive behavior. I don't mean to suggest that physical aggression is justified and therefore allow-able, but I encourage parents to observe and reflect. Make clear distinctions between doing and feeling, acting aggressive versus verbalizing angry feelings. Most children will respond positively to being listened to and having their feelings understood. Of course, if despite all these efforts, the behavior persists for months or grows worse, seek the aid of a trained child counselor.

Along with making your behavioral expectations clear, offer many opportunities for children to express their feelings, including anger, in acceptable ways. Pretend play with toys and dolls is a fine vehicle even for chil-dren who are quite verbal. Storytelling and drawing with accompanying narrative also works well. It's fine if your child has one doll hit another doll, since it is "just pretend." It helps not only to be unfazed by any sort of pretend play content, but also to join in, always allowing the child to direct while you translate her action into words. "Oh, I see the bear is very angry at the giraffe. I wonder why." Some anger will be dis-sipated if she senses you understand and accept her feelings, even if you won't allow harmful behavior to real live people or property.

My Discipline Approach Isn't Working

Q: My three-year-old son is so aggressive some-times that it's frightening. I am at my wit's end about what to do. If I smack him for being naughty, he hits everyone else or himself or me. I have tried being nice and loving, and he gets even worse. What can I do?

A: *Children learn a great deal about how to behave by watching what we do.*

I can't be as confident about suggesting what you should do as I am about recommending what you should not do, namely smack him or use any form of punishment that you wouldn't want to see him put into his own behavioral repertoire. Children learn a great deal about how to behave by watching what we do. So it would be wise to eliminate all displays or threats of physical aggression. I could not hazard a guess about what may be the basis of his anger at you. Sometimes children this young expect the primary parenting person to be able to control everything in the world — so in his mind, if you really wanted to, you could give him whatever it is he wants. Those expectations are very likely completely unrealistic. To help matters, as well as get a possible hint about what is bothering him, try giving him one hour a day of your undivided attention — time when you play together, following his lead. See if having you to himself and being the boss of the play eases his frustration, and watch for hints in his pretend play. The only rules are that no one be put in harm's way and nothing be destroyed. You may discover amazing confusions acted out with toys. If this approach does not achieve your goals in a few weeks, ask your doctor or school for a referral to an expert in early childhood mental health. It may not take much time for the expert to help you and your boy get on a more congenial track.

Controlling Children's Behaviors

Q: My two-and-a-half-year-old daughter is still wearing diapers. I want to force her into potty-training by having her start wearing panties. She loves the idea of panties, but we have had no luck making her go on the potty. Any suggestions?

Q: When I try to get my three-year-old to eat different foods, he cries and cries. Right now, he eats grits, eggs, and cheese on weekends or cereal for breakfast. His lunch is a grilled cheese sandwich, banana or peaches, and maybe some vanilla pudding. And for dinner, he has hot dogs, pizza, or a grilled cheese sandwich, peaches and banana, or sometimes shrimp fried rice. I can't make him eat any vegetables or any other meat. Please help!

Q: My four-year-old won't stop sucking his thumb. What should I do?

A: *Forcing isn't possible.*
One of these questions is about potty-training, one about food struggles, and the last about thumb sucking, but they all have something important in common. They are based on the premise that parents can and should force kids to do or not do things relating to the children's own bodies, the way the parents want. Well, that just isn't the way things work with healthy, robust children.

To the parents of the two-and-a-half-year-old who is still not intrigued enough about wearing panties to do things her parents' way: Trust in your child's under-standing of her own readiness to use a potty. From time to time, continue to offer those nice rewards, and when it happens (and it will happen), enjoy bestowing them. If you make too big a fuss, even over success, though, she could wonder if she is still in charge of her own body.

To the parent who is concerned about nutrition: Of course, consult your pediatrician or family doctor. He or she will probably recommend making certain foods available, introducing new foods gradually, but not forcing them. Many young children are not adventure-some when it comes to trying new foods, and that's okay. It is far better than initiating a power struggle, which no one wins.

Similarly, we can't force a child to stop thumb suck-ing. To that parent, a kind warning: If you try, he will only dig in his heels. So instead, seek opportunities to engage him in fun and interesting activities, allow him to be the leader when you two play, and enjoy every chance to praise him when he does something grown-up. He will suck his thumb as a soothing activity until he no longer needs to or is too busy having age-appropriate fun.

In all of these situations, forcing not only doesn't pay off; it isn't even possible. I suggest taking the exactly opposite tack—using your adult wisdom to figure out what might motivate your child to move toward the behavior you seek, on his own.

My Daughter Is Defying Me

Q: I am a single mother having a difficult time deciding the right way to discipline my three-year-old. She will not eat fruits and veggies, does not listen to me in situations when I tell her no, and sometimes she yells back at me. What should I do?

Q: Time-outs don't work with our three-year-old because she won't sit still unless someone holds her or yells at her — and then she dissolves into tears. If I put her in her room, she stands at the door and bangs and screams. In fact, I think she would break the door if I didn't hold on to it. Yes, she is defiant but she is also very creative, artistic, affectionate, and so tenacious. I don't want to break her spirit — only curb it somehow.

A: *Don't let this little person engage you in battles for control.*

The mother of an almost three-year-old told me the following story: Her daughter had done something exasperating so this mother instituted a five-minute time-out. The girl complied, but when her mother asked her, "Now, do you understand why you had to sit there?" Her response was clear: "Yes, Mommy. I had to stay still until you felt better!"

Raising a spunky young child has its trying moments, for sure. And if time-outs work, it may be at least in part because they give parents or teachers time to collect themselves. But when you feel better, think of the bright side. These two little girls and many others like them are wrestling with a core human conflict — the urge to be safe and therefore compliant and the equally powerful urge for autonomy. At this moment in their development, the drive to be in charge seems to be winning, but the balance will tip either way at different developmental phases.

To both of these parents: Try to keep in mind the potential life benefits of your daughters' tenacity and determination, and then it should be easier to avoid power struggles. Pick your battles very carefully — making the single standard for nonnegotiation the safety of all concerned. Otherwise, don't let this little person engage you in battles for control. In fact, encourage the inclination for independence by giving your daughter choices whenever possible (of course, of two or more things that are equally agreeable to you). Put your foot down when you really must, but otherwise enjoy the emergence of this increasingly competent person. And above all, model the kind of behavior you hope she will adopt.

To the parent whose child is refusing to eat certain foods: Offer fruits and veggies and take them away without comment if they are rejected. If nourishing food is always available, she'll get what she needs over time. Your daughter wants to decide what goes into her mouth and tummy. Testing out her will against yours is her first practice run-through of self-care and a defense of her bodily integrity. Even arguing and negotiating, annoying as it may seem, have great potential benefits in learning to think logically. So stand your ground in those few matters that require your protective wisdom. Otherwise, try to enjoy the daily test of your mettle. You'll need the practice to get ready for her preteen years.

Too Old for Tantrums

Q: My four-and-a-half-year-old daughter has many wonderful qualities, but recently she has started having major tantrums. (I thought she had outgrown this sort of behavior quite a while ago.) Now, she becomes defiant and sometimes even hits. I try to react with a firm voice and a negative consequence, but that often creates a bigger problem. I have noticed other girls in her class with similar defiance issues and other mothers who say, "This behavior is unacceptable." But no consequence is given, and the behavior continues. I want my daughter to understand what is acceptable behavior, but I don't want to be an overly strict and unforgiving parent. What should I do?

A: *Positive consequences for appropriate behavior.*
You have eloquently described a dilemma shared by many parents: How do I set limits without doing harm to my child's self-image or to our relationship? While there is no universal answer, finding one, in this situation, would probably involve observing and listening carefully to discover what may be behind the recent outbursts. Ask yourself if there might be something going on in her world that could have incited her regression to toddlerlike behavior. There are so many possibilities. Some of the more common ones include

the birth of a new sibling, conflicts between parents or other family members, a move, a loss (even if it is a loss of control over previously taken-for-granted realities), or adult expectations that exceed her ability to comply. Since you say that a number of other children in her class are behaving similarly, I wonder if there is something about their current school experience that is making unrealistic demands. If your daughter continues to express her anger this way, have a chat with the teacher to see if he or she has any clues. The one who truly holds the answer, of course, is your daughter herself. Try spending at least a half hour a day playing with her, allowing her to take the lead in dramatic play — maybe playing school or switching parent/child roles with her or allowing stuffed animals to do the role-playing.

While you are waiting to acquire insight about the origins of the problem, give your daughter as many opportunities as possible to make appropriate decisions, such as whether to have peanut butter or bologna for lunch, whether to read this story or that one, etc. Treat her with respect and model the respect you expect from her in your interactions with others. Stick to your principles about the way people should treat one another, but eliminate the negative consequences. All the data we have suggest that positive consequences for appropriate behavior are much more effective than negative ones for inappropriate behavior.

Preoccupied with Death

Q: My three-and-a-half-year-old daughter is preoccupied with death. I think it began when we were talking about pets we had had before she was born. She asked where they are now, and we said they became old and died and are in heaven with God, and having fun, even though we miss them. In her pretend play, my little girl speaks about things like "the mommy died" or "the doggy died" and seems very worried. We have told her that most people live to be old and that we hope to live to an old age and meet our grandchildren and maybe great-grandchildren. (We are somewhat older parents.) Now we have started to make sure she is not around when we watch the news. And I have tried to be matter-of-fact in my answers to her questions, but she may sense that the questions disturb me. I would welcome any suggestions.

A: *Let her know that you understand what she is feeling.*

You are obviously a very caring, sensitive parent and doing everything you can to be honest, yet reassuring to your child. Your story brings to mind the often quoted poem from Ecclesiastes about there being a time for everything, a time to live and a time to die, etc., and the fact that, unfortunately, life does not always follow that ideal plan. What is more, some real events, and talk about them, may turn out to be ill-timed in terms of any given child's developmental work. Your daughter is apparently bright, sensitive to the world around her, and struggling with her first awareness of mortality. You are very wise to eliminate all TV and radio news in her presence. And since she is so very astute, I would suggest that you also try to eliminate adult talk about sick friends and relatives and any allusion to your seeing yourselves as "somewhat older" parents. You see, you have told her that you expect to live to be old, but when is that? It could be tomorrow in the mind of a three-year-old, especially since she has probably heard you say that you are already older. Bright as she is, the subtleties of old and a little old and a little older escape her. I am not implying that you should shut the door on any question or any concern of hers; in fact, it is helpful for you to let her know that you understand what she is feeling. Don't discourage the pretend play that expresses those feelings, but you can inject a note of optimism, a happy ending here or there. While parents are advised to accept and acknowledge their children's feelings, they can put an optimistic spin on things by showing confidence in their own ability to care for and protect their children, come what may.

All families go through changes. At the very simplest level, new members are born, they grow older, and eventually die. Along the way, some marriages break up, new marriages occur, and families may merge. In this chapter, we talk with parents about how to help their children accept inevitable change with minimal strain.

Can a Mother's Pregnancy Affect Her Child's Behavior?

Q: My kindergarten-age child has quit doing his work at school, and his teacher suggested that my pregnancy may have something to do with this sudden change in his behavior. I disagree. We never talk about the upcoming baby at home, so how can a baby that is not here yet be a problem?

Q: My eight-year-old son (who has two younger brothers and a new baby on the way) has been sucking his two middle fingers and rubbing anything that is silky since he was a year old. This happens when he is at school, home, church, going to bed, etc. We are now questioning if we have let this habit go too long. Should we step in? If so, how? It just seems that eight is awfully old for this to be going on all the time.

A: *Be open about the expected newcomer.*
Both of these questions mention an expected new baby, which neither parent considers a factor in her

child's behavior. Before I state my hunch to the contrary, let me hasten to say that parents who enlarge their families are *not* being disloyal or unkind to the children they already have. But not every older child sees things so reasonably. If we suspend our own reasonableness and consider what it feels like to be either of these first children, we may get a greater understanding of what is going on.

Looking at the questions, it is certainly possible that the change in the kindergarten child's behavior has little to do with the pregnancy. There could be something going on in the classroom and all possible explanations should be explored. But, for the moment, let's consider whether not talking about the baby coming is the best way to keep it from being an issue. I don't think so. The baby is an imminent reality, and not talking about it could make that fact seem ominous. Any bright, alert five-year-old could be wondering what it will be like, what it will mean for him, whether he will still have a place in the family, or even why his parents would want another child if they are satisfied with him. So I would suggest being open about the expected newcomer. Encourage freedom to play and draw and chat about it. When the time seems right, talk about the importance of being a big brother. While the baby will be pretty "boring" for a while, not able to play or talk or catch a ball, gradually his big brother can teach the younger child so many things. Welcome whatever the first child may want to ask or say directly, or indirectly through imaginary play, and make him a part of fun planning, baby room decorating, high-chair painting, etc.

The second parent asks about a child who may have a strong, though not atypical need for physical closeness and reassurance. He already has two younger siblings and another one on the way. As a toddler, he learned to comfort himself in a perfectly acceptable way — sucking fingers and feeling something silky soft. It is possible that each new baby's arrival or anticipation has evoked that same yearning and response. I understand the dilemma about whether to step in and actively discourage the finger sucking, but I would advise a different tack. Show this boy lots of affection. Highly praise everything he does that you genuinely do admire. Day in and day out, reward him with your loving smile and a hug for age-appropriate jobs well done. Allow him as many oldest-child privileges as possible, staying up a half an hour later, for example, and offer frequent invitations to assist with grown-up tasks. In other words, guide him toward his own discovery of the perks of being an eight-year-old, rather than an infant. After all, you can't beat getting affection, attention, and big-person privileges, too.

Divorce Is Powerful Stuff

Q: My ten-year-old daughter was recently diagnosed as having ADHD. She had been an interesting child to parent since birth — very creative, sensitive, and intelligent. Her teachers recommended testing her for entrance to a program for the gifted in kindergarten. But lately, my daughter has had a difficult time conforming to school rules about waiting to speak until called on, staying in her seat, etc. Her dad and I have been in the process of getting divorced. He strongly objects to her taking the medication that was recommended for ADHD, and he has demanded another opinion through his lawyer, who forbids using the medication until that opinion is heard. My daughter feels this is all her fault. She is more anxious and edgy than ever. I tell her she is not to blame, but that doesn't work. How can I help her to have some peace?

A: *You have a common interest in the well-being of your daughter.*

Is it possible that the recent symptoms, which seem to suggest ADHD, are simply signs that a very bright and sensitive child is, as you suggest, deeply troubled by the conflict between her parents? All too often, children become an innocent battleground for warring, divorcing parents. I would suggest calling a truce, while both of you seek counseling on behalf of your child. The counselor should be an experienced child, family, and adult psychiatrist or psychologist, who can avoid taking sides, except for the child's. If at all possible, that same counselor can also work with you and your ex-husband pointing out that you have a common interest in the well-being of your daughter. Anything that could persuade you to work toward a calm, mutually respectful divorce would be most likely to save your daughter from further pain.

I have seen the benefits when both divorcing parents do rise above the temptation to battle and the lingering suffering for their children when they don't.

Ultimately, your daughter may also benefit from an opportunity for sustained counseling with her own therapist.

What Is the Best Custody Arrangement for a Toddler?

Q: My husband and I are separated. He wants to take our twenty-month-old daughter to see his parents, who live halfway across the country, for eleven days. I'm okay with the idea of her seeing her grandparents, but my daughter and I have never been apart. My husband had not shown much interest in the baby until the separation. Now he also wants to have her for 50 percent of the time. He doesn't have a suitable living arrangement and doesn't know much about how to care for a young child. I want my daughter to know and love her daddy, but I think she is too young for the arrangements he wants. Am I wrong?

A: *Stand your ground.*

As I see it, you certainly are not wrong. Your family finds itself in a sad situation that has become all too common. While a father can be just as fine a primary parent as a mother, if they separate, one or the other should be the consistent primary parent in these early years. That is what bodes best for healthy emotional, social, and even cognitive development. Not only is eleven days far too long for you and your baby to be separated, any kind of fifty-fifty custody arrangement is not recommended for at least the first three years.

For the time being, it would be best to leave your child only for a few hours at a time, only in familiar surroundings, and only in the care of a loving, familiar, competent caregiver (including her father). So I recommend that you stand your ground, but not through a confrontation with your husband. Instead, go through an attorney, whose argument would be bolstered by the consultation and advice of an expert in child development and infant mental health. A neutral expert should have an opportunity to explain to your husband and you why it is essential for every child to be able to rely on the presence of her primary caregiver in these early years. This mental health professional can appeal to the one thing that you and your husband still have in common — a genuine wish to do the right thing for your child.

Your husband's family might travel to where you live to visit their granddaughter while she is so young. Her daddy should be encouraged to have frequent visits, allowing him to develop a relationship with his daughter that can grow in the days and years ahead.

Concerns About Sleeping Arrangements

Q: I am divorced and the father of a very precocious six-and-a-half-year-old boy. He is really a delight, congenial and easy to guide. I enjoy my several regular visits a week with him enormously. We talk a lot, and I recently learned from him that his mother still has him sleep in bed with her, except when a boyfriend stays over. This is worrisome to me. Am I being foolish?

Q: I have been divorced for four years and have custody of my seven-year-old daughter. My ex sees her several times a week for a couple of hours, and for one full week in the summer when they go out of state to visit his parents. This will be the third year they will go on that trip together, but one thing is very different this time. He has remarried and intends to have my daughter stay in the same room with him and his new wife (although they'll be in separate beds). I think that's inappropriate, especially since my daughter hasn't even met the new wife. My daughter is uncomfortable with it, but can't bring herself to tell her father. And he doesn't understand why I have reservations. Is my opinion so out of line?

A: *Stand your ground.*

In my view, neither one of these parents is foolish or out of line. In fact, both are right on target. Unfortunately, there are times when some divorced parents have difficulty putting the best interests of their children ahead of their own needs. Although it is unwise to make a bed companion of a child to assuage loneliness, some parents do it. They forget that the child may suffer from such intermittent closeness, which depends only on the parents' needs. And, of course, sharing a bedroom with a newlywed parent and his wife is likely to be equally unsettling.

All that is clear. The question that I can't answer is what either of you can do about it. You might suggest consulting an impartial third-party expert — a child psychologist or psychiatrist, a clergy person, even a mutually trusted attorney who could direct you to someone familiar with the needs of children. Depending on how strong your feelings are about this, you could, of course, return to the legal locus of your divorce. In any case, I wish you luck in your efforts to defend the best interests of your children.

Dating Again

Q: I am a single mom who is ready to start dating again. How can I prepare my children, who are seven and eleven years old, for a new chapter in their mom's life? And if a new relationship becomes serious, how do I explain that to them?

A: *Go slowly.*
My response to your important question can't be very specific since I don't know the circumstances of your single status; that is, among other things, whether you are widowed, divorced (and how long ago), or have always been single, and whether the children both have the same father. I also don't know whether you have ever before brought a date home to meet either child. So my answer cannot be tailored to your precise needs, but perhaps a general discussion of single-parent dating could be helpful to you and others in a similar situation.

I would advise you to keep your social life separate from your family life until you feel confident that the relationship is a serious one and likely to last. That is because you wouldn't want your children to suffer the loss of another father figure. Secondly, when you do introduce the idea that another person has come into your life, prepare the kids by saying you would like them to meet a good friend of yours. Invite him for a meal or to an outing that includes only the four of you. Give the children time to get used to the idea of that upcoming event, not to mention the importance of this person to you. Go slowly. Don't expect the children and your friend to become instant buddies. Rather, expect each child to have her own feelings about the new situation. Their reactions will vary based on temperament and age, among other things. An easygoing, affable child is going to react quite differently from a wary one. Be patient and prepared for the fact that children in this situation typically have mixed feelings. If they are still in touch with their biological father and/or hoping for a reunion, they may see the existence of this new guy as a threat to the family's ever reuniting. Children of divorce do often hold on to that wishful fantasy. They may also wonder if they are being disloyal to their own father if they enjoy being with your friend. But above all, they might fear you will love this person more than you love them. And if your friend has his own children, that adds another dimension to the challenge, including sharing you and their possessions with these "interlopers." Don't expect that having a heart to heart about it all will end the worries. It will take time and probably some rocky days before everyone is at ease.

When Life is Stressful

Q: Our five-year-old preschooler has been through so much in his short life. My husband is in the service, and we recently moved back from two years overseas. On the way, we traveled to see members of my family, who live in another country. Then our dog, who had been with us since before my son was born, was killed by a car. And now my son has a new baby brother, and his daddy is away a lot for his new assignment.

It seems that my son is handling everything just fine, but I am worried because he doesn't talk much about the dog, the friends he had in our old home, the grandparents, aunts, uncles, and cousins he met, or why Daddy isn't home much. His teachers say he is doing very well in school in all ways, and he seems happy to me, too. Is it foolish of me to worry?

A: *Your son feels protected by his relationship with you.*
You are describing a child who is apparently quite resilient. I agree that any one of the stresses you mentioned could at least temporarily have affected many children. And we know that stress accumulates, for children and adults. Experts in child development have been studying children like your son. In some cases, they have followed a large number who had many early life stresses, monitoring them from birth until they reached their thirties. As it turns out, about one third of those children have done fine, despite it all. This is very interesting for us to learn because the next question is: What is it that makes those kids resilient?

If we knew the answer, we could perhaps help all children to acquire similar immunity.

Obviously, we don't have all the answers yet, but we do know that one powerful positive influence that protects kids from stress is having even one adult person in their lives who is there and believes in them. In the ideal case, that is a parent such as you. Of course, that is not by any means the whole story, and parents who are very supportive may still have children who, for many reasons, including basic temperament, lack this level of resilience. But it does seem likely that your son feels protected by his relationship with you.

That leads me to the second point I wanted to make. Very often, when we ourselves feel stressed, we expect our children to feel the same way. All of these changes must have been very difficult for you. First, you leave a home you have made your own for two years. Then you see family from whom you had earlier been separated and you have to separate again; you lose your dog — because it was your dog, even before your son was born. And now you have a new home, a new baby, and a husband who is not around much to help. You have no friends nearby yet, and probably not much time to make new friends.

My advice is to seek the support you need, perhaps through your husband's branch of the service. Many service families are in similar situations, and counseling is available. If you can afford to call old friends and family — even if it is a little over your budget, allow yourself that, too. If you have a computer available, send e-mails to stay in touch. And when your husband is home and the moment is right, discuss it all with him — being sure that he doesn't think you are blaming him. He may provide some of the support you need, even if it is necessarily intermittent right now. It seems that both you and your son are strong enough to get through this rough time, but you both are entitled to the support that he already feels he has.

Talking About the Death of Someone Close

Q: I don't know whether or how to tell my six-year-old daughter that we lost a very good friend of ours. Some members of my family think I should spare her, but the news will have to come out sooner or later, especially since we saw a lot of this family friend. Can you give me some advice?

A: *Kids should hear the simple truth right away.*

I agree that there is nothing to be gained by hiding the news. It probably isn't even a good idea to postpone telling your daughter. Secretiveness can sometimes make bad news seem even more menacing. Another benefit of telling your daughter the truth is that it provides an explanation for your downcast mood, which might otherwise be puzzling or troubling to her. Keep your explanation simple, saying that you are sad (so that she knows it is okay to be sad after a loss). In language she will understand, make it clear that this was a very unusual event since it occurred in a young adult. She may or may not start to ask pointed questions about what happened or what could happen to members of her own family, whether they will get sick and die soon. You can't promise not to die, but you can point out all the reasons to be optimistic about your living a long, long time.

When a parent, sibling, or grandparent to whom a child has been close dies, surviving adults face an even greater challenge. But once again, kids should hear the simple truth right away. They may react in many ways, all of which are normal — such as a short-lived shedding of tears, followed by an apparent indifference or silent denial of the news. Remember that children mourn differently from adults. While it is a good idea to let some of your own sadness be seen, don't expect your child to respond similarly. She may return to play, to school, to everyday life, as though she didn't have a care in the world. That does not mean she is heartless or not mourning.

Soon after a death in the family, allow kids to express their feelings, but don't expect them to do so. Let them know that you are open to listening to their thoughts or questions whenever they are ready. But don't push. Regressive behavior, such as aggressiveness, tantrums, losing recently acquired self-controls, whining, and irritability, is to be expected. Kids should be allowed to attend the family's ceremonies if they choose. It is a good idea, though, to have an adult available to take them away if they need a break.

CHAPTER FOUR — ABOUT SCHOOL AND LEARNING

School and education have a growing significance in children's lives. Learning success is associated with life success in our society. In this chapter, we look at the pressures on kids and their parents to succeed and how they each can begin to cope.

Really Early Readiness

Q: I am six months pregnant with my first child and very eager to do anything/everything I can to help my child's mind grow to its full potential. From an educational point of view, is it beneficial to allow the baby to hear music while still in the womb? Should I continue throughout her infancy? Should I read to her while in the womb? What age is okay to begin teaching her to read? I would greatly appreciate any advice you could offer.

Q: I have a sixteen-month-old-girl, and I am wondering what the right age is to teach her to count and to learn her ABC's. I want her to be ready to do well in kindergarten.

A: *The best preparation for academic learning is falling in love with the world.*
   I wish you could hear my deep sigh when I read these two earnest parents' questions and many others like them. I do so admire the commitment to do whatever may help their children to succeed, but I am dis-

mayed about the messages our culture has imparted about how to accomplish that. Of course, it is fine to play good music when the baby is in or out of the womb, and to read to her as well. But there is nothing magical about doing so. There has been some theorizing about music and brain development, music and math, but the jury is still out on the specific benefits of prenatal and postnatal exposure to music or reading. We do know that babies recognize and prefer the sounds of their own mothers' voices when they are even a day old, and that they will choose to hear other sounds that are familiar, including music. My guess is that the sound of a mother's voice reading tenderly to her unborn child could begin the important work of attachment that precedes and accompanies the communicating and relating necessary to thrive and to learn. So I urge both questioners to do what they enjoy — listen to their favorite music, sing nursery rhymes, read their favorite children's books, but adult books, too, if that is what they like to do.

In other words, start to share who you really are with your baby — have fun relating and listening. Help your newborn to fall in love with you and the world around her, but take your lead from your child. When she has had enough interacting, allow her to rest, and even turn away. Be responsive to her needs, even while enabling her to adapt and be calm. I know it may be hard to believe, but the best preparation for academic learning is falling in love with the world — developing the desire to explore and to know. Offer your child age-appropriate opportunities, for example, a soothing music box, a mobile over the crib, but most of all, the reliable sight of your face, smiling and encouraging her, in infancy. For toddlers, look for toys that allow the exercise of new skills like walking and talking, but always the fun of interactive play, which can't be beat.

There is no good time to formally teach ABC's or counting in a didactic way. Instead, incorporate these things in everyday age-appropriate play. Sing the ABC song tenderly; count the three duckies on her bib; and later, read instructions aloud, count the number of crayons offered, and name their colors in passing. Ask your child to give you two blocks when you are building together, or to find the toy behind the green lamp. Use these words in everyday conversation. "Oh, look at Clifford, the big red dog. And he has two doggie friends." As time goes on, model the behaviors and lessons you want your child to acquire — be a reader yourself, relax with music, and be responsive and loving, even while setting necessary limits for your children. Offer opportunities for social interaction with other children, but don't expect instantaneous politeness and generosity. Demanding that or didactic teaching of letters, numbers, or reading when a child is not ready for it can have negative effects — even turning a child off to such learning. In other words, your love is enough when it is reliable, responsive, and full of opportunity to grow at the child's own pace.

Separation

Q: Our four-year-old son is having a terrible time adjusting to preschool. We spent two hours letting him meet the teacher and explore the classroom the day before school began. The next morning, he was eager to go to school, but fell apart when we were leaving. We visited for lunch, as promised, which started the crying cycle again. I've talked with him about his apprehensions, and all he can say is that he wants me with him or he just wants to be at home. The school advises that I drop him off and not come back till pickup time. Is this really the best thing to do? It seems akin to throwing a child into the pool and letting him figure out how to swim.

A: *Separating from home and family for the school day is a daunting task.*

At every season of the year, parents write to me with concerns about their young children's troubles with separating. One parent may say, "He starts crying two hours before the school day begins, but stops (the teachers tell me) five minutes after I leave him there." Another parent may write, "She doesn't want to stay without me, but when I pick her up, she doesn't want to leave school to go home." There is great surprise and disappointment on the part of those parents who say, "I don't get it. Last year was a breeze. She's in the same school this year and cries and cries about not wanting me to leave her there."

In some cases, a child does just fine in the first few days or weeks of a new school experience, then suddenly balks about going or pleads with Mommy to "please stay with me." Similar experiences are reported after vacations or following children's absences because of illness. And separation issues frequently arise when there are concurrent changes at home — a new baby, a move, divorce, or other family loss.

Your situation, however, is the most common of all. As always, it helps to understand what is going on in the mind of the child, although, we can't ever know that for sure. For most preschoolers and many early primary-grade children, separating from home and family for the school day is a daunting task. And it's not that they absolutely don't want to do it. In fact, there is a real conflict between the urge to be independent and "big" enough to separate and the fear of not being entirely safe without family. There are strange adults and noisy unfamiliar children in a room that seems enormous or worlds away from comfort and safety. But then again, there are all those toys and a child or two with a friendly face. It's all so sudden, though, and bewildering. Where is the bathroom? Where is the door that Mommy will walk back through? What if I want juice? What if I can't do what the teacher wants me to do? What if she doesn't like me?

Children know what we all know: They can't fend for themselves yet and instead depend on the protection of loved ones. It's no wonder that many, if not all, young children are uneasy about starting school. Wise teachers and parents have devised many ways of reassuring them and of supporting the urge for independence. Many preschool programs have gradual entry: a few children at a time for a shortened day with a parent present. And even before that awesome first day, many good programs have school visits by one child and parent at a time and home visits by teachers. Parents have the opportunity to tell what they know about their children's special likes, dislikes, temperament, and habits. Preschoolers, especially, are encouraged to bring security symbols from home — a special blanket, a stuffed animal, or photos of the family that can wait in the cubby for whenever they are needed. And ideally, a parent is encouraged to stay and observe for as long as he or she is needed; parents are urged never to leave without saying good-bye, maybe even with a special ritual of good-bye kisses and hugs. For many parents, much of this recommended gradual separation is difficult or impossible to arrange with work schedules or younger children at home. Compromise may be possible — another relative or close friend might stay when the parent can't. The more respectful parents and teachers are of each child's rate of readiness to separate, the more respectful and interactive they are with each other — staying in contact, playing with the child together early in the day — the sooner a child will feel safe enough to enjoy increasing independence and the wonderful resources of the classroom, not to mention new friends.

If your child protests or cries, it's not his failure or yours. It is a way of saying, "Work with me and the teacher. Give us time, and we'll do fine."

Sitting Still at Preschool

Q: My three-year-old son's day care tells me that he has a difficult time sitting still. Even while concentrating on a task, he stands up, sits down, and stands up again. What can I do to help him?

A: *Children this age are full of energy.*

Unless there are other unreported behaviors that might arouse concern about your son's development, I would surmise that he is doing just fine. What is not fine are the inappropriate expectations of important adults in his life. Anyone who is a professional caregiver for three-year-olds should understand it is absolutely expectable that children this age will be full of energy. Of course, they will often move from sitting to standing and back again. I would wonder about a child of three who comes to day care and sits quietly doing what teachers in elementary school call seat work for long periods of time. Just like puppies and kittens, young children are bubbly, bouncy, and playful. It is unrealistic and even unkind to ask them to be otherwise. Such expectations can, at times, result in a child's feeling puzzled, sad, or angry about not being able to please grown-ups. Then, *really* worrisome behavior could follow.

If the child-care provider cannot tolerate normal three-year-old behavior and provide lots of positive feedback to a child who apparently concentrates well, it is time to consider another arrangement. Remember that it's important, too, for young children to have many opportunities for free creative play, rather than adult-designed "academic" or even formal projects.

Kindergarten Readiness

Q: I am concerned about my four-year-old daughter who now attends preschool three half-days a week. She is eligible for kindergarten next year, but our school district just decided to make kindergarten a full day, and I don't think my daughter will be ready for that. Her birthday is near the cut-off date; she is timid, quiet, and very tired when she comes home from her half-day program. She was a premature baby and was eligible for speech therapy as a toddler. When she was three, I was told she was developmentally normal. I am wondering if I should keep her back a year or send her to a private half-day kindergarten. What do you advise?

Q: My daughter turned five last August 31 and began kindergarten a few days later. Her teacher has told us from the beginning that she is highly intelligent but not mature. She is the youngest in her class — in some cases by ten months. We are trying to decide whether she should repeat kindergarten. If so, should she go to a different school to avoid her current classmates? Would she benefit more from staying in familiar surroundings if she stays back? We also worry that she may become bored since her scholastic capacity is even high for her current class placement. Any advice would be welcome.

A: *Is this school ready for your child?*
  I do wish that parents and children were not put in the uncomfortable position shared by these two

families. Perhaps I can be of some help by sharing the results of current research as well as many child development experts' shared opinion on this matter. Most of us in the field are convinced that the appropriate question to ask is not "Is your child ready for kindergarten?" but rather "Is this school ready for your child?" In other words, is the school willing to meet each child where she is and provide the educational and social opportunities she needs to grow? All too often, the school simply expects each child to conform to standards. Since both of the questioners here have indicated that changing schools is a viable option, it is one to consider.

As for the research findings, it is interesting to note that despite common assumptions to the contrary, there is scant, if any, evidence that the age a child is when beginning elementary school has a genuine effect on academic performance. However, I propose that the teacher's and parents' knowledge of the birth date of some younger than average children can become a self-fulfilling prophecy of school problems, or a ready explanation if anything doesn't go perfectly smoothly.

There is another unexpectable but consistent finding: Children who are held back a year before entering kindergarten are much less likely to have later school problems than comparable children who repeat kindergarten. There is much speculation about why this should be the case, including the notion that a child and family may experience a sense of failure about repeating a grade, even kindergarten, and in the eyes of the school community, it can be seen as a negative mark as well.

With these facts in mind, I advise the first parent to seriously consider not sending her child to the full-day kindergarten next year and, instead, research the availability of alternatives. At the same time, she should consult an expert in early childhood, preferably one who is a child psychologist or child psychiatrist with training in infant mental health. I say this not because I think, from what she relates, that her child has a serious problem, but because I think the parent herself should be helped to abandon her assumption that her child is forever fragile because she was a preemie. The timidity of the little girl is probably partly an aspect of her innate temperament and partly the counterpart of the parent's understandable concern. Obviously, I am going out on a limb even saying this much, since I do not know the family or the school situation, but hopefully this will provide food for thought.

As for the second question, first I wish I knew what "not mature" means in this case. Knowing the specifics about the child's behavior would help a lot in advising. So, once again, I would suggest that a consultation with an early childhood expert, as described above, and one not associated with the school, to assure objectivity, could be most helpful. I would not be put off by the early birth date itself. But since the school has taken this tack of labeling the child as "not mature," I suggest looking for another program that is willing to work with the child's strengths and her less developed areas as well, to enable her to be productive and happy with school and herself.

Is Your Child's Teacher Right for Him?

Q: My son, who turned six in December, is having problems in school. He is good in math, but the teacher says he is far below grade level in reading and writing. He is very shy and his confidence is low. I know that he can read most of the words he learns at school, but the teacher says he refuses to read and she is not able to find out how much he knows. My son doesn't want to speak about school. How can I help him? What should I do?

A: *Is this class ready for him?*
First of all, I don't think you should allow the teacher's comments to create worry about your son's innate academic ability. Think about it. How far below grade level can a child who just turned six be? Ideally you should be replacing the question about whether any child is ready for kindergarten or first grade with the question, "Is this class ready for him?"

The school should be obliged to meet children where they are, guiding each at his own pace, allowing each and every one to be and feel successful. No wonder your son doesn't want to talk about school. His confidence is shaken by the cookie-cutter expectations of a program that does not meet him where he is and guide him toward success. Try having a talk with the teacher. After you listen to what she has to say, assess for yourself whether she is able to be more flexible. Get a sense of whether she herself may be the victim of pressures to "reach standards." I am afraid that many of the newest trends in measuring kids and indirectly measuring teachers can take an awful toll on kids' potential joy in learning. Why don't you try speaking to the principal about observing other teachers at your son's level. Perhaps there is a classroom where your son will be more appreciated. Or, if there is any way to do so, consider transferring him into a program that is not bound by these pressures. In the meantime, do fun things with him yourself in relaxed situations and find valid reasons to praise his accomplishments again and again. Let him know you admire and believe in him.

My Child Is a Slow Mover

Q: My son's teacher says he is the slowest-moving student in his first-grade class. He takes the longest to get his coat on and finish his projects. She concedes he is extremely bright and does superior work, but claims she and the rest of the class are getting "disgusted" with his "pokey" attitude. She also claims he has a medical problem and needs to be put on medication. I do not see any indication of a medical problem. What do you think?

A: *Very bright children have very high standards.*
I have to take a deep breath and a slow walk around the block before answering your question: It

so distresses me to hear stories like yours. The teacher's name-calling and enlisting of your son's classmates as co-critics is indefensible and compounded by her stepping out of her role as teacher to make an unfounded medical judgment. I am not sure how you can discreetly go about it, but you may need to enlist the help of the school principal. Don't accuse or attack the teacher; just let the principal know that you are puzzled about why a teacher would want to embarrass a child, rather than guide him and his parents toward more adaptive behavior.

There may be many reasons for your boy's slower than average pace. He may be not only unusually bright, but also a perfectionist about his work. Some very bright children have very high standards and are inclined to interpret assignments in far more complex terms than were intended by the teacher. He may also become so engrossed in the work that time gets away from him. Psychologists who have studied the performance of children and adults who are totally engrossed in areas of great interest have praised this sort of total concentration.

This wouldn't, however, explain your son's slowness in dressing to go outside. What is more, both the good news and bad news about educating gifted kids in a regular school setting is that they need to adapt to the expectations of an average classroom. The good news is this might help to prepare them for the real world, and the bad is it could discourage some of their complex problem solving and creativity.

I suggest that you consult with a child psychologist who is an expert at evaluating ability and personality style. Hopefully, you will get a sense of your son's intellectual potential and current functioning. You'll also get insight about his way of relating to people and their expectations. Finally, a child psychologist or child psychiatrist can recommend ways to help your son enjoy his gifts, while also adapting to the demands of the world around him.

CHAPTER FIVE — WHEN TO CONSULT AN EXPERT

Parents have so many concerns about how they and their children are doing. Sometimes all that is needed is informed reassurance, but there are other times when expert intervention is essential and can help. In this chapter, we consider the difference between what can be seen as normal child development and the likelihood that it is time to get help.

Is This Normal Behavior or ADHD?

Q: My son is three years old and extremely active. He talks nonstop and gets very angry when we ask him to wait his turn to talk, or stop talking to eat, listen, or go to sleep. We have tried time-outs and taking things away. Nothing works. He still wants his way and is very impatient. Yet he can sit and play with a toy, or watch a show he likes for more than thirty minutes at a time. He has an active imagination, and is extremely loving and gentle when he is not frustrated. Does he have ADHD?

Q: Shortly after my now eight-year-old son entered kindergarten, he was diagnosed with ADHD. At about the same time, his father and I got a divorce. Since all this happened, he has been going to counseling once a week and is progressing well, but he is also very sensitive and can't handle anyone talking to him in a stern way. If he thinks you are angry with him, he will either shut down or lash out. Is this because he has ADHD?

A: *Be careful about labels.*

ADHD refers to an official diagnostic category in current use: Attention Deficit Hyperactivity Disorder. (The term *ADD* is no longer in use by mental health professionals.) I, however, believe that more often than not, perfectly understandable behavior on the part of young children is mislabeled as ADHD. In fact, this seems to me to be reaching the proportions of a cultural obsession, which stands in the way of our truly understanding what makes children tick. Unfortunately, it is very easy to find a professional who will label a child of any age as having ADHD with no more evidence than the fact that his energy is overwhelming to the adults around him. When that happens, the child is stuck with the label, whether it is accurate or not.

In answer to the first question, many three-year-olds talk nonstop and balk at taking turns or sharing anything, including the podium. There is no value in punishing or labeling them for just being three-year-olds. Of course, it is up to us to patiently and gradually communicate our expectation that they learn to take turns. As this parent points out, hers is a child who can concentrate and sit still for things that intrigue or interest him, without even being told to do so. A three-year-old who loves to practice his growing skill with language, who is egocentric, as is developmentally expectable for someone his age, who has a fine imagination, and who is often loving and gentle does not "have ADHD."

The eight-year-old, who presumably had difficulty sitting still and concentrating when he was in kindergarten and whose parents were going through a divorce, has since calmed down and responded to the support of a counselor and is not a likely candidate for the ADHD diagnosis, either. Yes, he is so sensitive to criticism that he either shuts down or becomes very angry. But most young children whose parents are divorcing are likely to have some impaired concentration, some anger, and some sadness. Everything that goes awry in a child's life and evokes unusual behavior does not translate into a justifiable diagnosis of ADHD.

Speech Concerns

Q: My son is three and a half and has a friend who is two days older. I can't help but compare the two. My son does not speak as well as his friend. He has had some speech therapy, and he is currently being tested to attend a special preschool. My husband and I work full-time, and when I get home, I try to talk to my son and find out how his day went, but it's sometimes hard to understand his answers. What else should I do to help my boy? I feel there is something more besides reading to him and discussing things with him. Is there any curriculum that I could use?

A: *Communicating and relating is what counts.*
No formal "curriculum" would be helpful. In fact, rote academic-style learning is not the way to go. You would do better to follow your instincts and good

common sense. You know there is nothing good that can come from comparing two young children's development. And it sounds as if your boy is doing great at relating and making every effort to communicate, despite some lack of clarity of speech. Communicating and relating is what counts at his age. The speech therapy and class for language-delayed three- to five-year-olds are all the formal learning he needs right now.

Be sure that his babysitter or teacher listens to him as you do, responds, converses, sings, reads, and interacts a great deal. Don't ask too many open-ended questions other than, "What would you like to play with me now?" Let him take the lead and you follow it, keeping a conversation or interaction going on his terms. When you are doing chores around the house, chatter to him about what you are doing, why, and what's next. Surround him with speech, acceptance, and love, and he'll be fine.

Stuttering

Q: I have a two-and-a-half-year-old son who has been stuttering for several months. The doctor says this is common, especially among little boys. The teacher at his day-care center said she has hardly noticed any stuttering at all. I am still wondering whether I should start him in some kind of early speech class.

Q: My two-and-a-half-year-old daughter who had been speaking and communicating quite clearly suddenly began to stutter. She catches herself, puts her hand to her mouth, and tries to correct herself, but struggles to get the word out. It breaks my heart. Is she anxious about something, or is it just a case of her brain moving faster than her mouth? Is there anything I can do?

Q: I have a five-year-old boy who just started kindergarten, and we have just moved to a new house in the same town. Recently, my son began to have a problem finishing a sentence without repeating his words three, four, and five times. He may say something like, "Mom, Mom, I want, I want, I want a, I want a snack." Is this just a temporary reaction to the recent changes in his life, or is something worrisome happening to his speech?

A: *Be calm and accepting.*
     As with almost all questions about growing children's behavior, speculations and explanations should take several things into account. The first is how long has it been going on, and the second is how common is this behavior among children of these ages.

The two-and-a-half-year-old boy's doctor is correct about how common and usually short-lived so-called stuttering is among children whose language is rapidly taking off. Then, too, it is surprising to me that no one has remarked about how advanced this boy is verbally, if he is speaking in sentences complex enough for the parents to notice stuttering. My guess is that his growth in this domain has been so fast that his early speech and his thoughts are not quite in sync. The same explanation probably applies to the girl whose parent inquired about her stuttering. The chances are that in both cases, the "leave it alone, they will outgrow it" school of pediatrics could be right. But to reassure yourselves, after having waited and watched for several months, why not take each of these children for evaluations by speech therapists who work primarily with young children? I don't mean to imply that either child should necessarily have speech therapy or join a speech class at this time. However, an expert in children's language and speech would be in a position to suggest what help, if any, is needed.

Remember, too, that we human beings are complicated creatures, so often several things can contribute to the same behavior. Common stresses — the birth or adoption of a new baby, a death, divorce, or other life change — coming at the time when language growth is quite rapid may influence fluency. What's more, parental concern can be contagious. So parents are advised to be calm and accepting, and not correct their child. Instead put an arm around your daughter if she is struggling, and with a warm smile, suggest that she take her time — letting her know that you are happy to wait and listen — rather than giving her a sense that you are impatient or finishing her thoughts for her. There is a greater likelihood of a problem resulting from worrying about the speech than from the temporary awkwardness.

Finally, the five-year-old child presumably has more developed language. In his case, as his parent suggests, the precipitating circumstance is more likely — the double stress of starting kindergarten (a major life event!) and moving to a new house. (Being in the same town doesn't lessen the stress of moving for a child, since his comfort zone is within the four walls of his family's home.) I would be less inclined to seek a speech evaluation at this time, and instead would encourage the family to offer lots of playtime together in the new home. Also, work with his teacher, keeping a close eye on his adaptation to the new school situation.

Limited or Delayed Language

Q: Our three-year-old daughter has very limited language. She uses few words, speaking mostly to ask for food or to tell us she needs to use the toilet. She shows no interest in learning the names of people or things, and won't listen to a story or to any request. Also, she can't seem to sit still. All this worries us because her older brother was able to do much more when he was half her age.

Q: My three-year-old has delayed language. He began using single words at thirty months, and even now uses very few sentences. Sometimes he makes funny noises when he is playing alone. We've also noticed that it's hard to get his attention.

A: *Delayed language development has many possible origins.*

Although there is very limited information available here about either of these three-year-olds, there is enough for me to share the parents' concerns. The good news is that both children do have some language. What's more, it's clear that the girl uses it to have some basic needs met, and perhaps the boy does, too. Those are positive signs. But delayed language development has many possible origins, some transient or otherwise insignificant, while others can be more serious. That is why it is essential for the parents of both of these children to seek a complete evaluation from a team of professional experts, including a child psychiatrist, developmental pediatrician, child psychologist, speech and language pathologist, and perhaps a pediatric neurologist and an occupational therapist as well. There is a federal law requiring all local communities to provide the funds for such evaluations and for whatever interventions may be recommended by the team of experts. This applies not only to school-age children, but beginning at birth, to every child whose development is atypical. Go to your board of education for information about how to get the process started. Of course, you have the option of seeking a private consultation with comparable experts. But don't put it off. Whatever the outcome of the evaluations, the sooner there is information and guidance available for you, the better the outlook will be for your children.

Developmental Delays

Q: Our four-year-old daughter is developmentally delayed. She has very limited language. In fact, our state's evaluation showed that the only area in which she functions at age level is her emotional and social development. The state provides both speech and occupational therapy, and she is in a class for preschool kids with language problems. My husband is very worried that she will have serious learning problems in the future. Although I am not happy about her being delayed, I feel that in the long run she will be fine. She is sociable, loves books, and is a responsive child.

A: *Play is vital.*

You put your finger on a very vital point. The fact that your daughter is a responsive child, is sociable, and enjoys interacting is wonderful news and bodes very well for her future. It is also good to hear that your state is providing the much needed speech and occupational therapy, which hopefully will be geared to your daughter's precise needs. If you and your husband continue to read to her and play with her, allowing her to take the lead, keeping two-way communications going back and forth, with spoken language, gestures, and facial expressions, her good spirit should continue. Having frequent opportunities to play with other children her age is also vital. I wonder, too, if she has been seen by a pediatric neurologist or a developmental pediatrician. Those experts along with a board-certified child psychiatrist or clinical child psychologist would be wise additions to her team.

I think that the best advice I can give you and your husband is to look at a book called *The Child with Special Needs* (Perseus Publishing 1998). Its authors, Dr. Stanley Greenspan and Serena Wieder, offer wonderful explanations and advice. You and your husband will discover that emotional and social development, notably a growing capacity to communicate and relate to others, should be the primary focus for parents and teachers of all children, not only those with developmental delays or special needs.

Is My Child Gifted?

Q: My four-and-a-half-year-old seems to be quite advanced for his age. His preschool teacher agrees, but we don't know how advanced he is or what to do about it. Our school district will only assess developmental delays. Here is some of what makes us think he may be gifted: He has been reading since the age of two and understands what he has read. He can do two-column addition without pencil and paper, and using the instructions from Lego sets, he can accurately build 100- to 150-piece models. He also installs his own software and figures out how to use it. He loves to problem-solve, and his eye-hand coordination is also advanced for his age. Is there something we should be doing for him?

A: *Help your boy enjoy his childhood and his gifts.*
If you live anywhere near a university that has a graduate training program for psychologists, I would recommend that sometime in the next year or so, you ask to have your son's cognitive ability tested in their clinic. The closer he is to six years old, the more stable and accurate the results are likely to be. Training programs have minimal fees, and you get the benefit of

several opinions, at the very least, the graduate student's and the supervisor's.

If you are able to consult a private child psychologist who does psychological evaluations of young children, that, of course, would be fine as well. But first think about and talk over with the clinician what the goal of the inquiry would be. I would imagine you will want some advice about how to guide and provide appropriate opportunities for your child. You are not simply seeking to discover a high IQ score or academic potential, but rather how to help your boy enjoy his childhood, his gifts, and life in general, make a responsible contribution to his world someday, and be a comfortable member of his peer group. You did not say anything about his social and emotional development or gross motor ability, but I am sure you would not want those important spheres to be overlooked. The consultant should be able to point you toward enrichment activities both within and outside of the school system, as well as social opportunities, and ways of combining the two. Whether a child is performing at age level, above, or below, whether she is gifted or talented verbally, mathematically, musically, artistically, interpersonally, or in any other way, she needs parents to tune in to her particular needs and provide loving guidance.

When Psychological Help Is a Must

Q: My six-year-old son has had terrible problems both in kindergarten and in camp. The teachers and counselors call it violent outbursts. When other children brush up against him or his things, and in his words, "pick on" him, he gets very angry and throws things at them, hits, and kicks. This has been going on for a while, and I don't know what to do.

Q: I have a twenty-one-month-old son. Two days after he was born, my mother died. I was devastated. I had no one to help with the baby, and I did a lot of crying. Two months later, I was diagnosed with cancer. I spent three nights in the hospital, unable to see my son. Since I received radiation treatment, I was not allowed to hold him for a while. Now he is so sad. He does laugh at times, but usually he is clearly unhappy. I am afraid I caused him to be depressed because I was so sad. I've been trying to make up for his early months by doing a lot of things together. Is there anything else I can do?

Q: My seven-year-old son has become afraid of our leaving him anywhere, including school and his grandparents' house. This is something pretty new, although he had always been a little unsure about people he wasn't used to and never has wanted to go to any friends' houses. When we take him to school now, the teacher has to hold him so we can leave. All the while he is crying and begging us not to leave him even in front of his classmates. The same thing happens when we take him to his grandparents. I am told he settles down after we're gone, but is very nervous the whole time about when we are coming back. We don't know what to do.

Q: I have a six-year-old boy who is very aggressive toward animals. He will pet the dog or cat very hard, and hit or push the creature down. His behavior borders on being cruel — purposely stepping on puppies, hitting, or throwing stones. This has been going on for years, and I feel I have tried everything. How can I get him to be kind?

A: *You and your child are entitled to have a consultation with an expert.*

Unlike most of the other parent questions quoted in this book, these cannot be answered with reassurances about age-appropriate behavior or typical reactions to real-life situations. The most responsible answer I can give to each of these parents is, "You and your child are entitled to have a consultation with an expert in child psychiatry or child psychology." Sometimes, with the best of efforts at parenting, through no one's fault, something goes awry. There are psychologists and psychiatrists who specialize in what is called infant mental health. This means they concentrate on the needs of children from birth to three years old and beyond, and work with parent and child together, in whatever way would be best for the particular parent-child pair. You can find one of them through the local or state mental health association, hospital, or national organizations such as the American Academy of Child Psychiatry, the American Psychological Association, and the Interdisciplinary Council on Development and Learning Disorders.

Any child can have a bad day, even a bad week that passes without our ever understanding why. But trends and patterns of extreme unhappiness deserve the help that is available in most communities.

CONCLUSION

These days, it is difficult to avoid comparing your child's progress with another's or with some arbitrary definition of standards. But do try. Remember, no two children develop at precisely the same pace. And most of the time, parents would do well to follow Dr. Spock's classical dictum: Trust yourself. You know your child better than anyone else. You know even better than he when it is time for him to sleep in his own bed, and that it is okay to express any emotion, including anger and jealousy, but not okay to act it out. And there are times when you would do well to trust your child himself to know when he has had enough to eat or enough sleep; to decide what he wants to play and with whom; to decide when he is ready to learn (to use the potty, to read, to separate from you for a whole school day, to play a sport of his own choosing); to know how he is feeling about himself, his world, and any changes in it.

There are periods in every child's life when it is wise to be especially vigilant, notably when there have been losses, or even ordinary changes — a new school, new community, new babysitter, new baby. At such times, children may feel powerless to do anything about what is happening, so you can expect brief regressions in their behavior. Try to tune in to their feelings and counteract the sense of being powerless by giving children choices that are harmless — what to wear (even if the choice is a plaid shirt with striped pants and a purple cowboy hat), what to eat (even if it is a steady diet of spaghetti and peanut butter), which toy to play with, or which video to watch (even if you have heard that dumb theme song five thousand times before).

If any problematic behavior persists, despite all your efforts, don't try to tough it out alone any more than you would if your child had a bacterial infection and there was a prescription for an appropriate antibiotic available from his doctor. As we have said throughout the book, there is expert help available for child-parent problems.

Above all, though, don't wait to become a grandparent before you relax and just have fun with those little miracles who can so enrich your life.

Books on Development:

Babyhood by Penelope Leach (Knopf, 2nd edition, 2001).

Behavior Problems in Preschool Children by Susan B. Campbell (Guilford, 2002).

Challenging Behavior in Young Children by Barbara Kaiser and Judy Rasminsky (Allyn & Bacon, 2003).

The Challenging Child by Stanley I. Greenspan, M.D., with Jacqueline Salmon (Perseus Books, 1995).

The Children's Hospital Guide to Your Child's Health and Development by Alan D. Woolf, M.D. Mph, et al. (Perseus Publishing, 2001).

Children's Play: The Roots of Reading by Edward F. Zigler, Dorothy Singer, and Sandra J. Bishop, Editors (0–3 Press, 2004).

Developmentally Appropriate Practice in Early Childhood Programs Sue Bredekamp and Carol Copple, Editors, (NAEYC, 1997).

Dr. Spock's Baby and Child Care by Benjamin Spock, M.D. and Steven J. Parker, M.D. (Pocketbooks, 8th edition, 2004).

The Emotional Life of the Toddler by Alicia Lieberman (Free Press, 1995).

The Essential Partnership by Stanley I. Greenspan, M.D. with Nancy Thorndike Greenspan (Viking, 1989).

Everything You Always Wanted to Know About Preschool— But Didn't Know Whom to Ask by Ellen Booth Church and Deb Matthews (Scholastic, 1996).

Everything You Always Wanted to Know about Kindergarten —But Didn't know Whom to Ask by Ellen Booth Church (Scholastic, 1996).

Everything You Always Wanted to Know about First Grade But Didn't Know Whom to Ask by Ellen Booth Church and Guy N. Fraser (Scholastic, 1996).

Learning and Growing Together: Understanding and Supporting Your Child's Development by Claire Lerner, Amy Laura Dombro, and Ross Whitaker (Zero to Three, 2000).

The Magic Years by Selma H. Fraiberg (Fireside, 1996).

The Mister Rogers Parenting Book by Fred Rogers (Running Press, 2002).

Playground Politics by Stanley I. Greenspan, M.D. with Jacqueline Salmon (Addison-Wesley, 1993).

The Trouble with Perfect by Elizabeth Guthrie, M.D., and Katy Matthews (Broadway Books, 2001).

What Do I Do When . . . My Children Don't Get Along? By Polly Greenberg (Scholastic, 1996).

What Do I Do When . . . My Child Won't Do as I Say? by Polly Greenberg (Scholastic, 1996).

What Do I Do When . . . My Child Loses Control? by Polly Greenberg (Scholastic, 1997).

Your Amazing Newborn by Marshall H. Klaus, M.D. and Phyllis H. Klaus, C.S.W. (Perseus Books, 1998).

Your Baby & Child: From Birth to Age Five by Penelope Leach (Alfred A. Knopf, 2000).

The Child With Special Needs: Encouraging Emotional and Intellectual Growth by Stanley I. Greenspan, M.D. and Serena Wieder, Ph.D., with Robin Simons (Perseus Books, 1998).

The Secure Child: Helping Children Feel Safe and Confident in a Changing World by Stanley I. Greenspan, M.D. (Addison-Wesley, 2002).

Touchpoints by T. Berry Brazelton, M.D. (Perseus Books, 1992).

The Yale Child Study Center Guide to Understanding Your Child by Linda C. Mayer, M.D. and Donald J. Cohen, M.D. (Little Brown, 2002).

Books on Special Issues:

Children and Grief: When a Parent Dies by J. William Worden (Guilford, 1996).

Through the Eyes of Children: Healing Stories for Children of Divorce by Janet R. Johnston, Ph.D., et al (Free Press, 1997).

Helping Your Kids Cope With Divorce the Sandcastles Way by M. Gary Neuman (Random House, 1998)

Being Adopted: The Lifelong Search for Self by David M. Brodzinsky, Ph.D., et al, (Anchor Books, 1992).

The Best Interests of the Child, Least Detrimental Alternative by Joseph Goldstein, Albert J. Solnit, et al (Free Press, 2000).

Associations:

NAEYC—The National Association for the Education of Young Children
1509 16th St., NW
Washington, DC 20036
1-800-424-2460
www.naeyc.org

APA—American Psychological Association
750 First Street, NE
Washington, DC 20002-4242
1-800-374-2721
www.apa.org

AACAP—American Academy of Child and Adolescent Psychiatry
3615 Wisconsin Ave., NW
Washington, DC 20016-3007
1-202-966-7300
www.aacap.org

AEGUS—Association for the Education of Gifted Underachieving
Students
P.O. Box 221
Mountain Lakes, NJ 07046
www.aegus1.org

National Association for Gifted Children
1710 L Street NW
Suite 550
Washington, DC 20036
1-202-785-4268
www.nagc.org

The Interdisciplinary Council on Development and Learning Disorders
4938 Hamden Lane
Suite 800
Bethesda, MD 20814
301-656-2667
www.icdl.com

Smart Kids With Learning Disabilities
www.smartkidswithld.org